GENTLEMAN CHAMPION

LEW OEHMIG'S
ROMANCE WITH GOLF

CHRIS DORTCH

FOREWORD BY WILLIAM C. CAMPBELL

CMD Publishing
Chattanooga, Tennessee
Copyright © 2001 by Chris Dortch

Gentleman Champion: Lew Oehmig's Romance with
Golf/Chris Dortch Foreword by William C. Campbell

ISBN 0-9709564-0-1

Book Design by Brian Hinchman

May 2001
FIRST EDITION

To order additional copies of this book, contact High Street
Management, 317 High Street, Chattanooga, Tennessee 37403
(423) 267-7040.

CONTENTS

FOREWORD

Having read the draft of Chris Dortch's book about Lew Oehmig and his legendary career, and agreeing with all the nice things said about Lew by all the well-placed sources, I can add little—especially as some of my own comments have been quoted. But I welcome the opportunity.

As many others have put it, nothing bad can possibly be said about Lew Oehmig. He is a favorite of anyone who has ever known him on or off the golf course. Nor do his friendly demeanor and courteous habits change with circumstances or the company he finds himself in. The most that can be said of anyone applies in spades to Lew—that he brings out the best in everyone around him. This is true both behaviorally, thanks to the good influences of Lew's example, and golfingly, as the simple mechanics and fluid tempo of his swing make the game look almost easy. In the process he has experienced far more victories than defeats, while treating both impostors alike; he is always a credit to the game.

I first saw Lew (without meeting him) when I visited a college friend in Chattanooga in the late 1940s and Lew was pointed out to me on the golf course as the local pride and joy. His sterling reputation as a golfer and person was confirmed in my getting to know him over the years—the proof being in the respect that everyone has had for him, and in his universal popularity, doubtless influenced by his consistently self-deprecating good humor. In all things he is the essence of civility and etiquette—and yes, proof that nice guys can win.

Unintentionally I tested Lew's friendly and gracious disposition in the 1980 Legends at Onion Creek in Texas, when we were the only amateur team in that better-ball event for which we had qualified as finalists in the '79 USGA Senior Amateur. The new One Ball Local Rule was in effect, so I had left in my golf bag only one type of ball—or so I thought, until discovering on the fourth fairway that I must have substituted a ball of another type, alas.

Upon discovering this Rules violation as I prepared to play to the green, I decided not to tell Lew until after he would hopefully have parred the hole for our better-ball score. So I merely suggested that he carry on without me, as he had two putts for "our" par. As luck would have it, and probably distracted by my strange request, Lew three-putted—without realizing that I was out of the hole, until I picked up my makeable putt for a presumed par-4. Only then did I tell Lew "the rest of the story," which might have infuriated a lesser man; whereas he only shook his head in dismay, and smiled.

His eventual all-time record of being the only three-time winner (and only six-time finalist) in the USGA Senior Amateur was symbolized by the three gold medals that are worn, in a vertical row hanging from a necklace, by Lew's devoted, delightful and attractive wife, Mary. Their combined weight must have been a mixed blessing for Mary, whose posture has thus been challenged. But she has borne the burden so gracefully that I couldn't resist lobbying Lew to win a fourth gold medal, the better to test Mary's ability to show them all off to maximum advantage.

Even before his amazing longevity as an outstanding amateur golfer was fully recognized, Lew's uniformly fine qualities were singularly celebrated by his selection in 1977 as the *only* U.S. Walker Cup captain who had not himself been a Walker Cupper. His faultless performance as non-playing captain of that USGA team was rewarded with his team's clear victory at Shinnecock Hills, where he was also well spoken— altogether, the ideal captain.

Furthermore, five years after his third USGA Senior Amateur title (at age 69—another record), Lew much deserved his selection as recipient of the USGA's 1994 Bob Jones Award. I had the honor and pleasure of making that presentation at the big dinner is Scottsdale, Ariz., a highlight of the Association's Annual Meeting. Lew's loving family were only the most obvious of his countless admirers who rejoiced that the right person was honored for a lifetime of distinguished sportsmanship—in his case, only an instinctive part of the man himself. So he was an obvious choice for the USGA's highest honor, reflecting qualities that Lew has shared with Bob Jones himself.

Even more than such widespread respect and appreciation nationally, the most impressive—to me—expression of Lew, the man, is his double-standing as both an accomplished golfer and a beloved person in Tennessee and Chattanooga, where he is known best. This happy truth was apparent at his 1991 induction into the Tennessee Golf Hall of Fame at a huge dinner inspired by the Honors Course founder, Jack Lupton, when Lew was honored along with his fellow inductee, Betty (Sparky) Probasco. These two great golfers and competitors had long been superb champions.

I was given the opportunity to present Lew; my wife, Joan, and I were grateful to be part of such a fitting and special occasion—when God was in his Heaven and all seemed right with the world.

In this same home town vein, Chris Dortch has done Lew proud with this biography, which I applaud as a well-written and warm account of a life well spent. I rest the case with a quote from the 1950s, that "with his stylish looks, smooth swing and friendly manner, Oehmig [is] a gentleman golfer." Indeed!

William C. Campbell
March, 2001

ACKNOWLEDGMENTS

An author's name might appear on the front of a book, but the process of researching, writing, editing and producing the work is far from a one-person job.

This I can say with absolute certainty after having written the book you now hold in your hands. The contributions of many people were instrumental throughout the life of this book, from its origins—it was conceived as a means whereby King and West Oehmig could honor the unparalleled golfing accomplishments of their father—to its final days in the hands of the printer and binder. I will attempt to thank those people here.

First, to King and West, thank you for asking me to document your father's life. As I learned in researching and writing this book, Lew Oehmig's accomplishments on the golf course were surpassed only by the number of friends he made along the way. If there is a central theme throughout this book, it's that Lew was as fine a gentleman as anyone could ever know. It was a pleasure to learn all I could about a man who touched lives more through his personality and character than his golf clubs. The similarities between Lew and his lifelong hero, Bob Jones, are dramatic, and not lost on those who knew both men. It was only fitting that Lew was awarded the United States Golf Association's highest honor, the Bob Jones Award, in 1994.

Without a doubt, many talented writers would have jumped at the chance to write Lew's biography. I appreciate King and West for choosing me for the task. And thanks go to King and West's mother Mary, Lew's devoted wife of more than 50 years. She gladly surrendered her scrapbooks and allowed me to take pictures off the walls of her home.

The efforts of several individuals were instrumental in my writing and research.

Thanks first to Sandee Jenkins, who edited my manuscript. Sandee had prior experience with golf history books, having edited *At the End of the Trolley: The First 100 Years of Chattanooga Golf and Country Club*, written by Susan Sawyer. I thought Sandee's experience would serve me well on this project, and it did. Her input was invaluable.

Another invaluable resource was Gene Pearce, who spent nearly two years writing and researching the definitive history on Tennessee golf. Gene spent countless hours in libraries across the state, digging through reels and reels of microfilm in his pursuit of old newspaper articles. It was Gene who sent me the first packet of newspaper clips on Lew, and thus jump-started my project. Because of Gene's input, this is a better book than it might have been. His vast knowledge of Tennessee golf history—of which Lew is an integral part—saved me many hours of research. I had the honor of editing Gene's work, and I can promise you that no state's golfing history has ever been as well documented. His book will be available through the Tennessee Golf Foundation, and if you have the slightest bit of interest in the state's rich golf tradition, I strongly suggest you buy it.

Speaking of the Tennessee Golf Association, I'd also like to thank its executive director, Dick Horton, for his help with this book. Like Nashville attorney and former Tennessee Golf Foundation director Lew Conner, whose own assistance to my cause was extremely helpful, Dick has long admired Lew Oehmig and was happy to share his recollections. Connie Pearce, Horton's valuable assistant, was also kind enough to let me go through the TGA's picture files and take anything I needed for this project.

Several other people helped my cause greatly.

Jeff Boehm, the unofficial historian at Chattanooga Golf and Country Club, willingly gave of his time and his vast collection of golf history books.

Rich Murray and Vicki Jonkers at the University of Virginia's sports information department opened their archives to me. Vicki was given the task of digging through years of old golf results, and she uncovered most of Mr. Oehmig's collegiate accomplishments.

Craig Smith, my friend and the media relations director at the USGA, was very helpful, as were all the folks in the USGA's library, who sent me clippings of Lew's numerous USGA honors.

Jim Ducibella, who wrote a fine history of Virginia golf, *Par Excellence: A Celebration of Virginia Golf*, was kind enough to share his manuscript with me. Ducibella's chapter on Sam Snead was important to my cause, for among all the professional golfers who competed against Lew over the years, it was Snead who became his closest friend.

Bill Campbell, former USGA president, Bob Jones Award winner and USGA Senior Amateur champion, is a long-time friend of Lew's who didn't hesitate in accepting my invitation to write the foreword to this book. He did a magnificent job, just as he did when he presented Lew for admission into the Tennessee Golf Hall of Fame and introduced him the night he was given the Bob Jones Award.

I'd also like to thank several of golf's governing bodies, including the Tennessee Golf Association, the Alabama Golf Association and the Southern Golf Association for directing me to various archival resources.

Thanks also go to Ira Templeton, Lew's long-time friend and golfing companion. Ira was gracious enough to allow me access to his scrapbooks and personal photograph collection. And he spent hours talking with me about his special relationship with Lew.

I'd be remiss if I didn't thank Brian Hinchman, a graphics and design specialist without peer who has helped me on several publishing projects. His excellent design on this book was the perfect complement to the words therein. The printer, Lithographics of Nashville, Tenn., did a fine job turning our efforts into book form. I knew Lithographics was our choice for the printing job when its representative, Eddie Brawner, began reeling off a list of Lew's golfing accomplishments, even before he'd read my manuscript.

Randy Parker, who has teamed with me on various golf-related projects over the years, is an excellent photographer whose work appears in this book. I thank him for his tireless efforts. I also thank my good friend and assistant editor at Blue Ribbon Media, Stan Crawley, for his help and encouragement.

Thanks also go to my wife, Patty, who has put up with me and my various sports addictions for a long time, and to my children, Chris II and Jennifer, for providing daily inspiration. I owe my parents, B.W. and Helen Dortch, a great debt, too, for giving me my appreciation for the printed word.

Finally, I'd like to thank the dozens of people who agreed to be interviewed for this book. Everyone I asked to speak about Lew was only too happy to do so. The mere mention of his name brought back fond memories for so many people.

In closing, I must point out that, at Lew's request, the net proceeds of *Gentleman Champion: Lew Oehmig's Romance with Golf* will be donated to the Tennessee Golf Foundation. That speaks volumes about the man whose life this book chronicles. Lew Oehmig has spent his entire life giving back to the game he loves so dearly.

Chris Dortch
March, 2001

CHAPTER 1

KILLING SNAKES

"Veteran Chattanooga golfers—the ones I have talked to—believe Lew Oehmig has everything except experience—big tournament experience. 'He should be the greatest player in the south in a couple of years,' is the way one expressed himself on the subject."
—Al Sharp in the *Chattanooga Times*, 1937

A s Lew Oehmig stood over a 15-foot birdie putt on the final hole of the 1985 United States Golf Association Senior Amateur, his opponent, Ed Hopkins, decided he had seen enough.

So Hopkins, a long-time friendly golfing adversary of Oehmig's, turned his back on his old friend, choosing instead to watch the Atlantic Ocean from just off the 18th green at Wild Dunes, near Charleston, S.C. Just as Hopkins feared, Oehmig, as he had done so many times in an amateur career that was by then in its seventh decade, summoned his God-given competitive spirit and calmly knocked the putt in the hole.

Hopkins didn't have to turn around to know that Oehmig had sent their championship match to extra holes. When Lew Oehmig needed a putt, really *need-*

Chattanooga Golf and Country Club, circa 1935.

ed a putt, he usually found a way to get the ball into the hole, even though putting was supposed to be the only chink in his golfing armor. And this was a putt Oehmig dearly wanted to make. History was on the line that day in 1985, for Oehmig, at 69 years old, was trying to win his third U.S. Senior Amateur championship, which no one had done before, oldest USGA champ in history.

Given the reprieve his clutch birdie putt had granted, Oehmig quickly took advantage. He won the championship with a par on the second extra hole, capping an incredible run in the Senior Amateur that may never be matched. Starting at age 56, Oehmig advanced to match play in 13 straight Senior Amateurs, playing in the championship match a record six times. Three times, he brought the trophy back to his home atop Lookout Mountain, near Chattanooga, Tenn., where one of the most impressive amateur golf careers in history began.

Reflecting on his final senior amateur victory 15 years later, Oehmig recalls expecting to win—not just that tournament but others that would follow. At 69, an age when most amateurs consider themselves lucky to be drawing back a club, Oehmig was still trying to win tournaments.

"After I won," Oehmig said, "I remember thinking that this could go on forever."

No one could have blamed him for that. Lewis West Oehmig had been playing high-caliber golf for a long time, etching his name into record books, earning his way into numerous halls of fame and—most importantly to Oehmig—making countless friends along the way.

The first anyone outside Chattanooga heard of Oehmig was in 1934, when, as an 18-year-old senior at the Baylor School, he beat Emmett Spicer, then Tennessee's finest amateur, in the Tennessee Amateur. Oehmig won his first state amateur in 1937, and seven more would follow, the last coming in 1971 at age 55.

A devoted family and businessman, Oehmig didn't consistently play a national amateur schedule until he reached his 50s. Thus, he didn't win a U.S. Amateur or play on a Walker Cup team, honors that surely would have been his had he competed in major tournaments every year. But he made up for lost time once he reached senior status, racking up two state amateur titles, seven Tennessee Senior Amateur championships, an International Seniors title and the three coveted U.S. Amateur crowns, to name but a few of his post-50 accomplishments.

Few golfing careers—professional or amateur—have been so successful for so long.

Oehmig's lifelong romance with golf, as his devoted wife Mary likes to call it, began in earnest in 1922, six years after he was born in Cincinnati, Ohio, the son of W.G. "Bill" and Ruth Oehmig. Lew was the second of four boys. The eldest, Von Daniel, was born in 1914. Lew was next in 1916. William G. III followed in 1919, and Dan was born in 1921.

The boys were naturally drawn to sports because of their father, who was a competitor in all walks of life. W.G. Oehmig was born in Rome, Ga., in 1880, and educated in Chattanooga schools. When he turned 21, Oehmig became involved in the life insurance business. Oehmig's work for Mutual Benefit Life Insurance Company eventually took him to Ohio.

Oehmig's life was forever changed there. He met Ruth Daniel, the daughter of a prominent grain dealer, in Cincinnati, and the couple married on Jan. 1, 1914. Von and Lew Oehmig were born in Cincinnati, but the family eventually moved to Chattanooga.

In Chattanooga, W.G. Oehmig, an avid sportsman and competitor, became dominant on the local tennis circuit, winning several tournaments, including the city championship. But after Oehmig was bitten by the golf bug, his tennis career was all but shelved.

"My dad had encouraged us to play golf even before he'd taken it up," Lew Oehmig said. "But when he did, he became so interested in it he read everything and absorbed all the knowledge he possibly could and passed it on to us. It was my dad who was responsible for my interest in the game and basic swing. He was just a real student of the game."

The elder Oehmig was more than just a student of the game. He became an excellent player, too. In the 1923 Southern Amateur played in Birmingham, Ala., Oehmig found himself paired against a young Bobby Jones.

The day before the match, Chattanooga police chief Ed Herron, who was also playing in the tournament and was a friend of Oehmig's, approached Jones in the locker room.

"Jones, I hope you wear your asbestos britches tomorrow," Herron said.

"Why's that?" Jones said.

"Because Bill Oehmig's going to burn your ass," Herron said.

Whether that comment was the catalyst that propelled Jones to future greatness is unclear. But Jones might have been a little miffed when he played Bill

Oehmig the next day. Jones won 8 and 7.

"After that my father and Bob Jones were always good friends," Lew Oehmig said. "That's how I got to know Mr. Jones. He was a fine gentleman, a great golfer and just a great person to be around. I don't recall specifically any wisdom he imparted to me. But I read all of his books. He was just a great example to me of what I wanted to be as a gentleman and a golfer."

The whipping handed Bill Oehmig by Bobby Jones did little to dampen his enthusiasm for golf. He was a competitor, and he passed that trait on to his sons, especially Lew, known throughout his golfing career as an intense competitor. The graciousness and friendly demeanor for which Oehmig also became known came from his mother.

"She was a real lady," Oehmig said. "Everybody who was associated with her loved her. She was very interested in gardening and had a beautiful garden. But she came out and watched us play every game, every golf tournament we were in. With four boys, it was tough to follow them all."

"Mrs. Oehmig was a jewel," said Scotty Probasco, a boyhood friend of the Oehmig brothers. "She was a very gracious lady and a wonderful person. Everybody just loved her. She was a true lady, a true Southern lady."

Though Bill Oehmig encouraged his four sons to play all sports, he thought that Lew, more slightly built than his husky brothers, might be better suited to play golf. To the best of his recollection, Lew played his first round of golf at age seven or eight. The family lived near Chattanooga Golf and Country Club, and when Bill Oehmig joined, his sons had a place to play and practice.

The country club, located in the Riverview section of Chattanooga, has a storied history. Established in 1896, the club was instrumental in helping form the Southern Golf Association at the turn of the century. In 1927, legendary golf course architect Donald Ross was hired to redesign the course. Two years later, the club became the first in the South to experiment with bent grass greens. The term "dog fight" was coined at Chattanooga Golf and Country Club when a member, overhearing a squabble that preceded the day's games, commented that it sounded more like a dog fight than a golf game. And the course played host in Oehmig's early years to several prominent tournaments, including the Southern Amateur.

"When a group of novice golfers founded the area's first golfing society in 1896, little did they realize their new club would not only survive, but thrive and prosper throughout the 20th century," wrote Susan Sawyer in *At the End of the Trolley: The First 100 Years of Chattanooga Golf and Country Club 1896-1996.* "From its humble beginnings at the end of the Riverview trolley line, Chattanooga Golf and Country Club has evolved into one of the South's most prestigious golf clubs."

Over the years, many of the game's great players came to Chattanooga Golf and Country Club to play casual rounds or exhibitions. The list includes Bobby Jones, Gene Sarazen, Ben Hogan, Byron Nelson, Cary Middlecoff, Sam Snead, Julius Boros, Gary Player and Arnold Palmer. The club produced several great players of its own, including four-time Tennessee Amateur winner Polly Boyd and Ewing "Pappy" Watkins, winner of the 1924 Tennessee Amateur and finalist in the 1920 Southern Amateur. The amateur that year was played at Riverview, and the winner was Bobby Jones.

Little did anyone at the club know when little Lew was swatting balls around with his sawed-off mashie that he would become the greatest player in the club's long history.

Young Oehmig was fortunate to be in close proximity to the country club.

"It was close enough to where we could walk or ride bicycles over there," Oehmig said. "There were any number of young guys out there that were playing golf."

Oehmig and friends such as Bill Voigt, John Fletcher, Jack Lovell and Billy Montague spent countless hours at the club, practicing and playing when they could. Occasionally, the country club's head professional, Wilbur Oakes, Sr., would pass on words of advice to the youngsters. Oakes had come from Scotland and was hired as the club's first pro in 1908.

He left a year later, but returned and served the club for 20 more years.

"My dad taught me the fundamentals," Oehmig said. "But Wilbur was very supportive of me. He was just a wonderful gentleman, very colorful."

Though Lew Oehmig was around golf constantly, his love for the game didn't come as quickly as it had for his father.

"I didn't feel like I was hooked," Oehmig said. "It was a subtle thing. I enjoyed playing golf, but I enjoyed other pursuits, too."

Oehmig and his brothers all played golf, but they had other interests. By all accounts, Von had a beautiful golf swing, but he was more interested in hunting and fishing. He also boxed, competing for the Dartmouth team as an undergraduate. Dan played football for the University of Virginia. Like Von, Bill III was also an outdoorsman, and he loved horses.

Ironically, it was a horse that might have convinced young Lew his future was in golf.

"We had a Shetland pony named Teddy," Bill Oehmig III said. "Every time Lew would get on him, that pony would throw his ass off. I think Lew thought golf was a little safer."

In time, golf became Lew's passion. As a young boy, he carried a mashie or niblick with him wherever he went. Sometimes the club served a dual purpose.

When Von Oehmig was 10, he came across a copperhead. Von called for eight-year-old Lew, who came running and quickly dispatched the snake with a deft swing of his club. It wasn't the last snake Oehmig killed with a golf club.

"... Then there was a much smiling Lew holding up a snake," wrote Al Sharp in the *Chattanooga Times* in 1937. "And he was taking it to his father. Telling him how he killed the four-foot snake with a mashie—a shortened mashie specially built for little Lew—while hitting flowers in an open field.

"And there was Von again telling about the time Lew killed another snake while on a vacation. 'Why, all he does is walk around swinging a golf club,' Von is saying."

By most estimates, six snakes lost their lives to the deadly mashie wielded by young Lew.

The Oehmig brothers, always close, were a fun-loving bunch. Scotty Probasco, who lived nearby and was a friend to all the Oehmigs, remembers the time the brothers played a Halloween prank.

"Our old house in Riverview had brick gateposts with these huge white gates hanging on them," Probasco said. "They must have weighed 600 pounds apiece. One Halloween, the Oehmig boys came and took the gates down and put them in the meadow. Dad calmly called Mr. Oehmig and said, 'Mr. Bill, could you get your boys to come back over and hang those gates up?' They confessed to me later it wasn't nearly as much fun hanging those gates up as it was taking them down."

The Oehmig family: Bill (rear), Von, Ruth, Dan, Lew and Bill

Lew Oehmig didn't focus on golf at Baylor. He also played football and basketball, excelling at both sports. He was a starter at quarterback and played guard for the basketball team. Clippings from both Chattanooga papers in the fall of 1934 prominently mentioned Oehmig's gridiron accomplishments.

"Lew Oehmig, who made quite a name for himself as a golfer here this summer, hurled a long pass that resulted in Baylor's opening touchdown, with flankman Jim Cowan on the receiving and scoring end," the *Chattanooga Times* reported after Baylor's season-opening 12-7 victory over Copperhill.

After Baylor's 21-0 loss to Tennessee Industrial, the *Times* was quick to point out that Oehmig didn't play.

"…The Tigers' city amateur golf champion, Lew Oehmig, regular numeral-crooner, watched the downfall from the sidelines. Lew received a lick on the back of the head in last week's gallop and was out by physician's orders."

When Oehmig started in golf, he wasn't as fortunate as junior players who would come along 60 years later and have a wealth of tournaments in which to play. Consequently, Oehmig had little tournament experience as a youngster, save his matches for Baylor. Few people outside Chattanooga knew of him or his steadily improving game.

All that changed in a two-week span in July 1934. First came the dramatic and improbable Tennessee Amateur victory over Emmett Spicer, for which the *Chattanooga Times* dubbed Oehmig, "Giant Killer." A week later, Oehmig won the first of his record seven city amateur championships, breaking Polly Boyd's three-year stranglehold on the championship. When Oehmig beat Dan Boone in a 36-hole final at the old Meadow Lake golf course, it announced the arrival of a new challenger to the old guard.

"Lew Oehmig, the 18-year-old golfing sensation from Baylor [simply fulfilled] a prediction that he was going to rise to the heights of Chattanooga golfdom when he made his way into the city finals," read a column in the *Chattanooga Times*. "... He was not expected to jump right into the niche made barren when Polly removed his form from the throne and packed his tourney clubs for the last time, but Lew got off with a flying leap and seems inclined to lose no time in making such prophecies truer than this grave soothsayer ever thought they would be at such an early date."

All that praise—and Oehmig hadn't even finished high school. He still had a year left; but long before his final year at Baylor was through, he knew his next destination: the University of Virginia.

Oehmig had been tempted by an offer from Rollins College in Winter Park, Fla., an NCAA Division II school that has fielded a strong golf program for decades. "Being down there in Florida really appealed to me, and I damn near went there," Oehmig said.

Before Oehmig could decide on Rollins, he got a little hard sell on the virtues of Virginia from Ed Finlay, whose family lived next door to the Oehmigs. Ed's son Ted was one of Lew's closest friends.

"Ted's father had been a big football player at Virginia," Oehmig said. "He'd told us it was a great school and a great place. So I decided to go there along with Ted."

Lew's decision would influence the lives of several of the Oehmig clan. Von Oehmig attended law school at Virginia after undergraduate work at Dartmouth. Dan Oehmig earned his law degree at Virginia. Lew's sons West and King attended the school, and King's son John is a student at UVa now.

Oehmig roomed with Ted Finlay his freshman year in Charlottesville, but the next year he moved in with Bobby Watts, who became the de facto golf coach. Virginia didn't have a full-time coach, so Watts was elected, for one important reason.

"He had a car," Oehmig said. "So we hired him to coach us. In those days, you had to drive to the tournaments. So Bobby was elected."

With a strong team that included Virginia state amateur champion Dick Payne, Walter Cushman and Bill Shannahan, the Cavaliers didn't need much coaching.

"We had just a helluva team," Oehmig said. "We were all scratch golfers when we got to the school. So we knew what to do."

Virginia's sports information department has no records before 1937, Oehmig's sophomore season. That year, he competed in six matches for the Cavaliers, compiling a 3-1-2 record. His best golf was ahead of him.

The following season, Oehmig was voted Virginia's captain, an honor he also held his senior year. His Virginia teammates were drawn to him, as would be

14

nearly everyone who associated with Oehmig through golf, because of his demeanor and outgoing personality. His ascension to team captain was practically a given.

"I'd like to think I was made captain because the other guys on the team respected me," Oehmig said. "I didn't have to take the job too seriously, though. We were all close friends. We knew how to win."

Oehmig made a lasting impact on several of his teammates.

"Lew was a senior when I was a freshman on the team," said Bill Battle, who would later become president of the USGA, presiding over golf's governing body through the Ping/square grooves controversy in the late 1980s and early '90s. "He was very influential in letting me participate as a freshman over some of the older boys. That was his decision as captain.

"We took several trips together, which to me were a great experience. We'd go up North in the spring and play Princeton and Swathmore and Penn and Rutgers. Lew was about as fine a model as you could have to follow. He was a great sportsman—always in a good humor but a terrific competitor. He had a very attractive personality and he was a terrific golfer with a magnificent golf swing. It all came together with Lew."

Oehmig's game came together at Virginia. After his second year, in the summer of 1937, he finally broke through in the Tennessee Amateur, beating Ed Falls in

Memphis at Colonial Country Club *(see Chapter 3)*.

"It's the greatest thrill I've ever had while I've been playing golf," Oehmig told the *Memphis Commercial Appeal*. "And I've been playing with golf clubs ever since I've been able to walk.

"It really was tough to have to beat Mr. Falls. He's one of the finest gentlemen I've ever played with. But, believe me, I'm certainly happy I won."

News of Oehmig's win spread quickly to the University of Virginia. "Cavalier Golf Team Gets Break This Year: They've Got Out Champion Oehmig," read a headline in the *Charlottesville Daily Progress*. The story was even more praiseworthy. "Oh, boy, the University of Virginia has something!" the story said. "Lew Oehmig, Tennessee State champ of golf, is on their golf team, and this makes Virginia the tops. Not many universities get a team like that—we expect Virginia to hit the high spots this year in golf."

Closer to home, the consensus among those who had seen Oehmig play or played against him was that he was bound for greatness.

"'He has everything it takes—temperament, the will to win, determination, the swing, the putting touch, all the shots, the strength to stand grueling matches, the physique—everything except a couple of years of experience.' Those were the words used by a veteran golfer to describe Lew Oehmig, Chattanooga's Tennessee state champion," wrote Al Sharp in the *Chattanooga Times* in 1937. ... "Veteran Chattanooga golfers—the ones I have talked to—believe Lew Oehmig has everything except experience—big tournament experience. 'He should be the greatest player in the South in a couple of years,' is the way one expressed himself on the subject.' "

Oehmig used his Tennessee Amateur championship as a springboard to a solid junior season at Virginia in the spring of 1938. Behind Oehmig's 13-0-1 record, the Cavaliers were also 13-0-1, an accomplishment that earned the team full athletic letters for the first time in the program's history.

Oehmig and Virginia qualified for the National Intercollegiate Tournament at Louisville (Ky.) Country Club in June, and Oehmig had high expectations.

A 2-over-par 73 left Oehmig one shot behind Michigan State senior Edward J. Flowers after the first round of 36-hole qualifying for match play. Oehmig shot a 72 the next day and tied Willie Turnesa of Holy Cross for medalist honors. A putt that hung on the lip at the 18th hole cost Oehmig the outright title.

In match play, Oehmig advanced to the semifinals before losing to Bert McDowell, an LSU sophomore, in 37 holes. McDowell had to rally for victory, squaring the match at the 36th hole and then knocking in an 18-foot birdie putt on the first extra hole for the win.

"The McDowell-Oehmig duel was a spectacular scoring affair," wrote Kenneth Gregory for the Associated Press.

Virginia was 11-2 and Oehmig 10-3 in 1939. Until he lost to Penn's Al Thompson in early April of his senior season, Oehmig had been undefeated in college. He eventually lost three matches as a senior. The Cavaliers once again advanced to the National Intercollegiate Tournament. The NCAA would begin conducting a championship tournament the next year, Virginia finishing 15th out of 21 teams as junior Dixon Brooke won the individual championship.

Oehmig's final college golf match was played at Wakonda Country Club in Des Moines, Iowa. After one round and a par 72, Oehmig was tied for qualifying honors with Vincent D'Antoni of Tulane and Rus Vifquain of Iowa State.

Things went badly for Oehmig after that great start. He shot 78 in the second round of qualifying, then lost 2-up to Mergle Getten of Minnesota in the first round of match play.

Thus ended Oehmig's college golf career. Though he wasn't able to break through in the national championship tournament, Oehmig's experience at Virginia was instrumental to the development of his game.

"My Virginia experience was a big part of my golfing life," Oehmig said. "Education was certainly important and the first priority. But the high-level playing experience and the contacts I made through golf at Virginia were invaluable."

As an underclassman, Oehmig was fortunate enough to come under the tutelage of Erie Ball, the head professional at nearby Farmington Country Club, where the Cavaliers hosted some of their matches and had playing privileges. Ball, from England, wasn't any ordinary club professional. The year Bobby Jones won the Grand Slam, 1930, he made the acquaintance of Ball at the British Open and asked him to come to East Lake Country Club in Atlanta. Ball didn't have to deliberate over the decision—his uncle Frank Ball was the head pro at East Lake.

Ball was a club pro his entire career, but found time to compete in major championships. He played in the first Masters in 1934, and also played in seven British Opens, 19 U.S. Opens and 19 PGA Championships.

"Lew and all of us learned by playing with Erie," Bill Battle said. "Not by being instructed, but just by watching. He was not a big man, but he had a magnificent golf swing—as pretty as you've seen anywhere. It was almost natural imitation."

"I learned a lot from old Erie Ball," Oehmig said. "Erie was just a wonderful player, a good coach and teacher and a real competitor. I still remember the things he showed me to this day."

"Lew had a good golf swing before I ever met him," said Ball, who at 90 was still giving lessons at Willoughby Golf Club in Stuart, Fla. "I just encouraged him to go with what he had. He was a great player, and had he wanted to, he could have gone on further to a higher level. He had one of the best swings of any amateur around in those years. I'm proud that I had a little bit to do with that."

It was through Ball that Oehmig met Sam Snead. Snead was a few years older than Oehmig, having been born in Ashwood, Va., in 1912. Like Oehmig, Snead was introduced to golf at an early age, but in a vastly different fashion. While Oehmig had Chattanooga Golf and Country Club—one of the South's finest courses—to help him hone his skills, Snead learned wherever and however he could. Often, he had to improvise, as Jim Ducibella explained in his fine book, *Par Excellence: A Celebration of Virginia Golf.*

"His first memories of golf start at age seven, when he'd go out into the fields and shag balls for his brother Homer," wrote Ducibella. "When the 19-year-old Homer balked at sharing his clubs with Sam, Snead had a plan. He tied an old club head to the end of a buggy whip and began swatting rocks around the property.

"Not long after, Snead cut a stick out of the woods, trimmed the knots and all but a dozen inches of bark that he used as his 'grip,' and attached another old club head. ...Unable to get onto the course to play, Snead took a couple of his mother's tomato cans and buried them in the pasture. Those became his 'greens,' and he spent hours hitting short shots at those cans, honing a wedge game that in later years was maybe the best in the business.

"To improve his driving, he'd wallop rocks or balls over fence posts on the farm. After a while, distance didn't intrigue him as much as accuracy, so he began aiming at the fence posts. Soon, he could hit them with regularity.

"And his famous draw was born out of necessity. On the family farm, there were mud puddles along the right side. If he hit too many balls over there, and came home too muddy, odds were he'd get a spanking."

As a boy, Snead caddied at the Cascades Course in nearby Hot Springs. He eventually became "club mate" at the course, and later got the big break his career was waiting for.

"In 1936, the Cascades Hotel announced it was hosting an 'open' golf tournament," Ducibella wrote in *Par Excellence: A Celebration of Virginia Golf.* "Snead entered and finished third, worth $358.66. Watching the tournament was Fred Martin, manager of golf at The Greenbrier in White Sulphur Springs, West Virginia.

"He offered Snead a job, only later admitting that he brought Sam to the resort with the idea of getting him the money to try the tour. It was the start of a relationship between Snead and the resort that exists even today.

"A year after accepting Martin's offer, Snead joined the pro circuit. The game would never be the same again."

As a fledgling pro, Snead would often come to Farmington Country Club to visit Ball. It was on a trip to Farmington that Snead met Oehmig, and the two young golfers developed a lasting friendship, playing many friendly rounds and exhibitions together. Though Snead was older and stronger, the two men were fairly evenly matched down to their swings, which were amazingly similar–their rhythm and timing was fluid and their action seemed effortless.

"Sam Snead's swing remains a classic example of simplicity and smoothness," wrote Dick Aultman and Ken Bowden in *The Masters of Golf.* "Its simplicity stems in large part from his coordination of movement."

As classic a swing as Snead possessed, many thought it was no better than Oehmig's.

Writing about the times Snead and Oehmig played together in his book *Tennessee Golf: Past and Present*, Gene Pearce brought up an interesting point.

"Who modeled whose swing after whom is a question that will never be answered," Pearce wrote.

As far as Oehmig was concerned, that was never a question.

"Certainly Sam's swing influenced me," Oehmig said. "I was a great admirer of his swing. The rhythm and the timing and the coordination were just so obvious."

Ball, who played a lot of golf with Snead and Oehmig, defers judgment. "Their swings were similar in that they were both graceful," Ball said. "I don't think Lew was as long off the tee as Sam. But if he wanted to turn pro, Lew would have been successful, just like Sam was."

Ball's contention can never be supported. Yet there was evidence in the exhibition matches Snead and Oehmig played that the latter would have been competitive against the best players on the PGA Tour. Snead eventually won seven major championships, 81 official PGA Tour tournaments and 14 more on the Senior Tour, more than earning his way into golf's hall of fame. And Oehmig always held his own against Snead.

"We took a few sheckles off him," Oehmig said. "Sam might deny that. I should have had his money framed. I always liked old Sam. I felt like we were good friends."

Of all the great players with whom Oehmig competed, it was Snead who became his closest friend. Oehmig maintained a lifelong admiration for Snead, and the feeling was mutual. Years later, Snead, in his typical direct fashion, made a statement that spoke volumes about Oehmig's game, especially as it related to the best players on tour.

"The best thing that ever happened to professional golfers," Snead said, "was that Lew Oehmig remained an amateur."

There was never much doubt that Oehmig would remain an amateur. After graduation from Virginia,

Lew Oehmig's father, Bill Oehmig

where he eventually earned a law degree in 1941, Oehmig's life would change drastically as he served in World War II, then began a business career and a family life. Professional golf was never a serious consideration.

CHAPTER 2

FAMILY AND
BUSINESS FIRST

*"I can't say that I ever seriously considered making
golf a vocation. I love it, but the strain must be terrific. And such a small percentage of the touring pros
actually wind up showing a profit."*

—Lew Oehmig,
in a *Chattanooga News-Free Press* story in 1956

Lew Oehmig was still a student at the University of
Virginia when he won his first Tennessee
Amateur championship in 1937. Much was expected
of the rising young star after that victory, but it was
another 12 years before he won his next state title.

Oehmig had his chances to win a second amateur
soon after the first—he lost in the finals in 1938 and
again two years later. But after a disappointing defeat
to Cary Middlecoff in 1940, Oehmig was a tad busy
for the next several years, busy with far more pressing
matters than golf.

In 1941, Oehmig graduated from law school at
Virginia. With a low draft number, he expected to be
chosen to serve his country in World War II, and he
was,—but not before he spent nearly a year working

George West, Lew Oehmig, Jack Lupton and Ira Templeton
at the Lupton City Golf Course in 1954

for Anderson and Clayton, one of the world's largest cotton brokers, in Houston, Texas.

Oehmig's budding business career was cut short when he was drafted in August, 1942.

Oehmig's first stop in his Navy career was Washington, D.C., where he served as an administrative officer in the office of the Vice Chief of Naval

Operations. Oehmig reported to Admiral Oscar Spears, whose family, coincidentally, was from Chattanooga. Spears' two sons, one of whom, John, attended Baylor, were lost at sea during the war.

Oehmig would soon encounter his own perils in the Pacific.

After his stint in Washington, Oehmig was sent to Hollywood, Fla., where he attended indoctrination school. "That really taught me something about the Navy," he said. From Hollywood, it was on to Pensacola, Fla., and Aerial Gunners school, then to Jacksonville, Fla., where he stayed for a year. At this time in Oehmig's life, golf was a distant memory.

When a friend of Oehmig's in Jacksonville was sent to Brazil to help train Navy gunners, Oehmig went with him. He quickly tired of that assignment.

"There wasn't much equipment down there, and nothing much to do," Oehmig said. "So I wrote the Navy Department and told them that I wanted to get out in the Pacific and fight the war."

Oehmig soon got his wish.

In late 1944, Oehmig was assigned to Air Group 10 and sent to Rhode Island to train. Oehmig was in Rhode Island for three months, then sent to the West Coast to train for another three weeks. Soon after came his final assignment of the war. Oehmig was to catch up with the *U.S.S. Intrepid* at Pearl Harbor. The ship's destination was Okinawa, where U.S. forces would make their final push against Japan.

Oehmig expected to see serious action, but nothing could have prepared him for what was about to happen. A report in the Navy's Office of Public Information archives picks up the story:

"Several serious enemy attacks were pressed home on 16 April, 1945, one [Japanese] plane managing to penetrate the task force screen at about 1336," the report said. "He had his choice. He chose *Intrepid.*

"Hit and trailing smoke, the kamikaze plunged into the flight deck in a near vertical angle, forcing the engine and part of the fuselage right on through. So great was the plane's impact that the exact imprint of its wings was smashed into the deck. A large hole was blown in the hangar deck by its bomb. Because of the crew's thorough experience in fighting fire, the gasoline conflagration was put out in a record 51 minutes. Eight enlisted men were killed, one was missing, and 21 wounded in this suicide blow, the fourth such attack *USS Intrepid* had endured."

Were it not for some quick thinking by Oehmig, more lives might have been lost on that tragic day.

"I was in the ready room with some of the pilots," Oehmig said. "There was great confusion in there, because smoke was rushing in from the west side of us, and we were blocked. We couldn't get out.

"Luckily, I was familiar enough with the ship and knew of a back entrance. There must have been a half a dozen people trying to get out the main door. I said, 'If you want to get out, you better follow me.' I took them out on a catwalk underneath the flight deck. We came out on the other side of the carrier and jumped up on the flight deck. The ship was weaving and sloping the whole way."

The badly damaged ship had to be sent back to the U.S. for repairs.

"Repairs to the flight deck were rushed, and three hours later *Intrepid* landed her planes," said the Navy archives report. "Commander Task Force 53 directed *Intrepid* to retire to the fueling area and investigate her damage and determine its extent. After a thorough examination the next day, the 17th, it was decided that *Intrepid* could continue in action only at greatly reduced efficiency. She was ordered to proceed to Ulithi for temporary repairs by an advance service squadron.

"Funeral services for the *Intrepid* dead were held 18 April on number two elevator. On 20 April the carrier reached Ulithi, and on the 215 service squadron technicians commenced tidying up the "Tough Old Lady," *Intrepid*'s sobriquet in the fleet. That she required more than temporary treatment was sadly apparent when previously undiscovered damage to the elevators came to light."

The events of April 16, 1945, were still etched deeply into Oehmig's memory, 56 years after the fact."We took a big hit," Oehmig said. "And we nearly lost the ship. But we survived it. We went back to the states, got the ship fixed and returned to finish the job."

As it turned out, Oehmig and his fellow *Intrepid* crew members didn't have to finish the job. On August 6, 1945, the atomic bomb was dropped on Hiroshima, effectively ending the struggle with Japan.

"The night we were getting ready to leave to go to Tokyo, they dropped the bomb," Oehmig said. "Needless to say, we were greatly relieved."

Though the war was over, it was several months before Oehmig returned home.

"My tour wasn't over," Oehmig said. "The air group made several show of force strikes against the Chinese rebels, who were trying to assert themselves. That kept us busy for a while."

Oehmig was eventually sent to Guam, where he served as an aide to Admiral Gunther.

"He was the top man in the Pacific," Oehmig said, "and a wonderful gentleman. He was from Memphis. I had known members of his family. Margaret Gunther, who was his niece, was a top-notch golfer whom I'd known before the war."

Oehmig stayed on Guam until 1946. Golf finally re-entered his life when he met Gunther's chief of staff, who was designing a golf course on the island.

"I wasn't there long enough to see it built," Oehmig said. "But I used to talk to him about holes and things he ought to include on the course. I guess they finally completed that course."

Oehmig didn't stick around Guam to find out. He was finally sent home in May, 1946.

Oehmig's life had been on hold as he served his country during World War II. At 30, he needed a job and some stability in his personal life. He found both in rapid order.

Oehmig will never forget a dinner party he attended on Lookout Mountain in 1946. It was there that Oehmig was re-introduced to Mary King, whose family had been friendly with the Oehmigs for many years.

"I'd known her for a long time," Oehmig said. "When we met again at that dinner party, something just clicked."

"We hit it off," Mary Oehmig said. "There was immediate chemistry."

In 1947, the couple got married, and soon Mary was joining Lew on his travels for the Coca Cola-Thomas Company, his first employer after his return from the war.

"Coca Cola-Thomas was the parent bottling company throughout the Eastern section of the United States," Oehmig said. "Mr. George Hunter was chairman, and he took me on after the war. It was a wonderful experience, traveling around, meeting people all over the Eastern half of the U.S."

Oehmig's job was marketing and merchandising.

"During the war, bottlers didn't have any reason to advertise," Oehmig said. "Our job was to help the bottlers get back to advertising and merchandising the product."

Oehmig's running mates in this endeavor, besides Mary, included old friends Carl Navarre, Ward Reilly, Jr. and Ward Crutchfield, who became a popular state lawmaker.

"It was a lot of fun," Mary Oehmig said. "They were all just college boys. It was a really diverse group."

The death of Mary's father, Henry King, sent Oehmig's career into another direction in 1948.

"After Mr. King had passed away, Overton Dickinson, Mary's brother-in-law, was called out of the Navy to run Mr. King's business, the Fleetwood Coffee Company," Oehmig said. "The company had grown rapidly. And Overton asked me to come work for the company and help him with marketing and other things."

In an inter-office memo dated Sept. 10, 1948, Overton Dickinson informed the employees of Fleetwood Coffee Company that Oehmig was joining the staff.

"It is with a great deal of pleasure that I notifiy you that we have been successful in obtaining the services of Mr. Lewis W. Oehmig, who will ultimately become sales director of our company. Mr. Oehmig was previously connected with the Coca Cola Company and will come to us with considerable experience in sales work. His connection with the company will date from Sept. 15, 1948, with the title of Assistant to the President. Mr. Oehmig will spend some time familiarizing himself with the operations of all other departments of the business. Mr. Oehmig will be introduced to all personnel from time to time as he passes from one department to another."

Oehmig excelled at his new job. And by this time he was again playing golf on a semi-regular basis. He returned to the local and state amateur circuit, where he once again competed for the Tennessee Amateur championship he last won in 1937. In 1948, the championship was played at Oehmig's home course, Chattanooga Golf and Country Club. Oehmig was qualifying medalist, but the tournament was won by a young and talented Chattanoogan, Wes Brown.

A year later, Oehmig finally won his second title, beating Memphian Jimmy Wittenberg, Sr., at Knoxville's Cherokee Country Club. Oehmig was once again on top of his game after a long layoff, but given the direction his business career was going, professional golf was not an option.

"Mary and I talked about it," Oehmig said. "But there was so little money in the purses. It didn't look very attractive, and didn't seem like the easiest row to hoe. They had Sam Snead and Byron Nelson and Ben Hogan out there. I'd played against some of them in exhibition matches. I knew it would be difficult."

In the late '40s, Lew and Mary settled into family life. A son, West, was born in 1949. Another son, King, was born in 1951.

After the boys were born, Oehmig never again considered professional golf, making him a gentleman golfer. With his stylish looks, smooth swing and friendly manner, Oehmig fit that role perfectly.

All the principals involved love to tell the story about the 1953 Women's Southern Amateur, which was played at Chattanooga Golf and Country Club. Before the tournament, the players were paired with men in a best-ball practice round. A young player from Kentucky, Betty Rowland, was teamed with Oehmig.

Oehmig's friend Scotty Probasco picks up the story:

"They started out on No. 1," Probasco said. "Betty had never met Lew. She was thinking he was an attractive guy with a nice golf swing, and that he hit the ball beautifully. He birdied No. 1 and left a birdie putt just short on No. 2. By this time Betty's thinking, 'My heavens, who is this guy?' She was just falling for him. And of course Lew was smiling and gracious, as he was to everyone.

"Going down the third fairway, which was then a par 5, Betty is still infatuated. About the time they were going to hit their third shots, a car stopped and out through the hedges came two little boys, screaming 'Daddy, Daddy.' It was West and King Oehmig, Lew's sons. And Mary, Lew's wife, was there, too.

"Mary told Lew, 'You ought to be ashamed of yourself.' And Lew said, 'What was I supposed to do, stand up on the first tee and say, 'Hello, my name is Lew Oehmig—I'm married and I have two boys?' "

Young Betty Rowland was disappointed at first, but she ended up finding her life's partner at that tournament. It was Scotty Probasco, who became his new wife's biggest fan as she became the female equivalent of Lew Oehmig. Like Oehmig, Probasco won eight Tennesesee Amateur championships. Oehmig's titles came in five different decades, Probasco's in four. Each earned the rare honor of serving as captain for a United States team in international competition, Oehmig at the 1977 Walker Cup matches and Probasco at the 1982 Curtis Cup matches. Both led their teams to victory.

Fittingly, Oehmig and Probasco were both charter inductees into the Tennessee Golf Hall of Fame in 1991. They were formally inducted on the same evening during a well-attended banquet in Chattanooga.

Oehmig began a remarkable string of dominance in the Tennessee Amateur while under the employ of Fleetwood Coffee, winning the title in 1951, 1952 and 1955. The latter victory tied Emmett Spicer's record of five championships.

In 1962, Oehmig won his record-setting sixth state amateur title, the victory coming over young star Bobby Greenwood at Chattanooga Golf and Country Club. That same year, Oehmig's career took another turn after Fleetwood was sold to Duncan Coffee, which was located in Houston, Texas. Oehmig stayed with the company for another couple of years while living in Chattanooga, but when he was asked to move to Los Angeles to run another Duncan plant, he politely declined. "I decided I'd rather stay in Chattanooga," Oehmig said.

Oehmig had plenty of options. Jack Harkins, a colorful, fast-talking Irishman and a member of Chattanooga Golf and Country Club, had started the Professional Golf Company in the '30s. Oehmig's brother Dan was a board member and legal representative for the company, and Harkins wanted another Oehmig in the fold.

"Old Jack had been after me for a long time to come over there and work with him," Oehmig said. "He wanted me to take over First Flight, which was the sales division of Pro Golf. I wanted to stay in Chattanooga, so I decided to do it."

Harkins, say all who knew him well, was quite a character. He led an interesting life, to say the least. He came to the U.S. in 1920, an Irish immigrant with $7 in his pocket. Living in Philadelphia, Harkins started a construction business before moving to North Carolina. There, Harkins became involved in a variety of enterprises. He was a pioneer aviator who enthusiastically piloted the old "Flying Jennies." Harkins walked away from four plane crashes. Obviously addicted to living life on the edge, Harkins also raced motorcyles.

He found a safer pursuit in golf, getting hooked on the game after beating three friends the first time he ever picked up a club. Harkins eventually went to work for the National Golf Company in Chattanooga, then, along with Chattanooga Golf and Country Club member Ewing "Pappy" Watkins, started the Professional Golf Company.

Harkins made his mark in the golf community of Chattanooga, with his playing skill (he had become a scratch golfer) and his boisterous, flamboyant personality.

Harkins had a flair for business, a gift of persuasion and an underrated knowledge of golf equipment design. In 1936, he developed the concept of swing weighting, which is still in use today. In the '50s, he introduced the steel-centered ball, which Harkins dubbed "Old Steely." The design concentrated the weight in the exact center of the ball for truer and longer flight.

Harkins was his own public relations firm, traveling around the country to try to convince players to use First Flight equipment. And he was successful, luring such stalwarts as 1950 PGA winner Chandler Harper, Doug Sanders and multiple-major winner Gary Player into the fold.

Eddie Davidson, long-time golf writer for the *Chattanooga Times*, remembers a meal he was invited to at the Read House.

"There were four or five of us at the dinner, including Gary Player," Davidson said. "When we were sitting around talking, Jack proposed to Gary the manufacturing of a Gary Player signature model club. I remember Jack telling Gary that if he signed with First Flight, he'd guarantee him $100,000. That was when $100,000 was a helluva lot of money. I think Gary accepted the deal at that dinner, and they went on to make the club."

Harkins died of cancer in 1964. After Harkins' death, Pro Golf and First Flight were merged into a single company. Later, the Arnold Palmer Golf Company, also started by Harkins, was merged into the mix. Oehmig recruited Jack Tucker, who had worked for Burlington Industries in Cincinnati, to run the newly reformed companies.

Tucker's ascension to power eventually led to Oehmig's departure from the golf business.

"Jack felt that with my position in the company, he didn't have the free hand he wanted," Oehmig said. "So he asked me to leave. Which I did."

Oehmig left Pro Group, which the company was then called, in 1972. After that, he could have faded quietly from the business world. Oehmig had long before started a development company with his three brothers, making several solid investments that could have provided for his family. But when old friend Scotty Probasco, then the vice-chairman of American National Bank and Trust, offered Oehmig a job, he couldn't say no.

"I didn't expect him to be a banker or anything," Probasco said. "I just wanted him to come in and frankly be a door opener and a builder of good will for us. Lew had his own business and his own money. I just made him an offer: 'I'll pay you a salary and give you your own desk and a base of operations.' He stayed with me quite a number of years.

"And it was a wonderful association. He got business for the bank. I didn't have him punching a clock. We encouraged him to play golf. Everybody loved Lew Oehmig."

"He was an excellent addition," said Ted Mills, one of Oehmig's oldest friends who worked with him at the bank. "He was just perfect for the job. Everybody loved him. He just fit right in with us and became a great asset to the bank."

Oehmig stayed with American National through some of his greatest triumphs in golf. He won the first of three United States Senior Amateurs in 1972, then won again in 1976. That year, Oehmig also won the International Seniors Championship.

"Lew was just a tremendous asset for us," Probasco said. "People knew him the world over. We hired him to open doors for business opportunities. And he certainly did that."

Oehmig stayed with the bank for more than 10 years, but even after he left he couldn't stay away from business. He started an investment company, 711 East Limited, with his sons. Well into his eighties, Oehmig tracked his investments in his home office with the help of the Internet. In 1984 Oehmig had been one of the very first users of a new computer called the Macintosh, and he has owned a Mac ever since.

Oehmig's refusal to stay idle was a key to his longevity, and helped explain his remarkable dominance on the golf course in a career that lasted several decades.

CHAPTER 3

TENNESSEE'S BEST AMATEUR

"Lew Oehmig added a touch of class to Tennessee golf. He was a true man of character, and I don't think there's anything better you can say about someone. But he was just as good a player as he was a gentleman. He was the tops. He was the best."
—Bobby Greenwood

The year was 1934, and one Lewis West Oehmig, an 18-year-old student at the Baylor School, was about to make his presence known on the Tennessee golf scene.

The occasion was the Tennessee Amateur. The venue, appropriately enough, was Chattanooga Golf and Country Club, Oehmig's home course, a place where he had played his first nine holes at age six. The opponent was the great Emmett Spicer of Memphis, a man who in the previous 10 years had won five Tennessee Amateurs and played in the championship match seven times. His duels with Chattanooga's finest players—among them Ewing "Pappy" Watkins, Pollack "Polly" Boyd and Darden Hampton, had become the stuff of legend around Riverview.

Little did anyone know when young Oehmig drew the 29-year-old Spicer in an early-round match that a new legend was about to start laying down roots.

Spicer, who had won the previous two Tennessee Amateurs—defeating Boyd at Nashville's Belle Meade in 1932 and L.P. Jones of Memphis at Memphis Country Club in 1933—was an exceptional player. From 1926 to 1933, he won five state amateurs, a feat that has never been matched. During that stretch, Spicer also won the Southern Amateur in 1926 and 1930.

"Emmett was the best player I ever saw," said two-time Tennessee Amateur champion H.P. Childress, who as a youngster caddied for Spicer. "He had a beautiful swing, and could hit a 2-iron as straight as an arrow. He once played an exhibition match against Bobby Jones at Memphis Country Club and Bobby told Emmett he was the better player that day, and that the only way Jones won was by making a few more putts."

Spicer had all the ingredients to be a champion, starting with his swing, which was fluid and powerful. So impressive was Spicer's motion that it inspired the man many consider the best player in Tennessee history, Cary Middlecoff, the Memphian who won two U.S. Opens (1949, 1956), a Masters (1955) and 39 tournaments on the PGA Tour.

"I was exceptionally fortunate that my original model was a great Memphis amateur named Emmett

Spicer," Middlecoff wrote in his book, *The Golf Swing*. "Right from the beginning—this was in the early '30s—I considered Spicer's way of hitting a golf ball basically correct. His was a graceful, easy style, and he hit the ball as well as any player I have seen since."

Spicer was also a fierce competitor, but he tempered that with a philosophy borrowed from the great Walter Hagen, as pointed out by Gene Pearce in his exhaustive history of Tennessee golf, *Tennessee Golf: Past and Present*.

"[Spicer] frequently quoted the words of golf legend Walter Hagen," wrote Pearce. " 'Don't forget to smell the flowers along the way.' "

Oehmig remembers being "intimidated" by Spicer in their 1934 Tennessee Amateur match, but somehow he managed to hold his nerves and his game together. Heading into the 17th hole, Oehmig had a 2-up lead. After Oehmig hit his approach to about three feet and Spicer's shot skipped across the green and into the fringe 40 feet from the cup, it looked as though the match was over.

Even Spicer seemed to acknowledge defeat—"by hastily jerking out a 3-iron," said an account in the *Chattanooga Times*—but it wasn't to come just yet. Barely studying the break for his downhill chip shot, Spicer made a pass with his 3-iron and sent the ball speeding toward the cup. It went in for a birdie. On the 18th tee minutes later, Spicer told spectators that was his "give-up" shot.

Rattled, Oehmig missed his putt.

"Naturally, I was shaken up pretty badly," Oehmig said. "I thought I'd choked."

The match proceeded to the 18th. While Oehmig sat waiting for Spicer to hit his shot on the 217-yard par-3 hole, he remembered a tip given him by his father. Newspaper accounts of the match tell of the youngster pulling out hairs on his legs, clumps at a time.

"That was from an old trick I taught my boys," Bill Oehmig later told the *Chattanooga Times*. "If you're nervous about anything, do something to inflict pain upon yourself. That relaxes you, just like getting hit the first time in a boxing match or making contact with the other fellow on the kickoff in a football game."

The strategy worked. After Spicer hit the green with his tee shot, which stopped about 20 feet past the hole, Oehmig stepped up with a 1-iron.

"The ball was high and perfect all the way," said a report in the *Chattanooga Times*. "And the crowd started cheering as it came down in a graceful arc, took the backspin on the green and stopped exactly hole high less than two feet to the left of the cup."

At that point, Spicer knew he was beaten. "Great shot," he said to Oehmig.

"Luckiest shot I hit in my life," Oehmig said 66 years later.

No one who watched him play that day attributed Oehmig's beautiful 1-iron to luck.

"I didn't think he could come back after missing that easy putt on No. 17," Spicer told the *Chattanooga Times*. "I thought I had him [after his improbable birdie at No. 17]. It took plenty of guts for the kid to come back like he did on No. 18."

Oehmig didn't win his first Tennessee Amateur in 1934. He lost his next match and had to watch as Scudday Horner of Nashville defeated hometown favorite Watkins for the championship. It was another three years before the Legend of Lew Oehmig would begin in earnest.

1937—The First of Many Championships

When Oehmig, by now a 21-year-old student and captain of the golf team at the University of Virginia in Charlottesville, finally earned his way to his first Tennessee Amateur championship match, he quickly made the most of his opportunity.

The 1937 tournament was played at storied Colonial Country Club in Memphis, and in the 36-hole finals, Oehmig was once again paired against a player several years his senior, 40-year-old Memphian Ed Falls. Oehmig wasted no time in building a lead during the morning round, winning the first hole with a birdie, the second with a par, the fifth with a par and the sixth with a birdie to go 4-up.

Falls sliced into the lead at No. 7 with a par to Oehmig's bogey, but the youngster won No. 9 with a par. He putted just 14 times on the front nine.

Oehmig finished the morning round in exciting fashion, making an eagle on the par-5 18th hole to eclipse a birdie by Falls. Oehmig reached the 500-yard hole with a 318-yard drive, gargantuan considering the equipment used in those days, and a 182-yard 5-iron that left him with a 12-foot putt, which he sank to take a 4-up lead heading into the final round.

On the day's 21st hole, Oehmig took a 5-up lead with a par. He went to 6-up with a bogey two holes later, and closed the match out with a par on the 32nd hole. The final score of 6 and 4 underscored the gap in talent between the two men, as Al Sharp wrote in the *Chattanooga Times*:

"Oehmig's brilliant golf—it was really brilliant for finals competition—in the morning made the big difference, you see, although I do not doubt that Lew could defeat Falls in every day in any week you name," Sharp wrote. "Falls, who said, 'I never took golf seriously and I still don't,' is a 75 shooter—a constant 75 shooter, as his Memphis foursome mates relate—and not a championship player as Lew Oehmig proved himself today in winning what might be logically termed his first major title."

Little did Sharp or anyone else present that day know how many more major titles Oehmig would win. Oehmig's family and support group who made the long drive to Memphis were just happy he'd finally won the Tennessee Amateur. It was the first victory in that tournament by a Chattanoogan since Darden

Hampton beat Ewing Watkins in 1931.

"There was Lew Oehmig, his face a deep red and his glasses twinkling in the late afternoon sun, sitting on the ground in front of the clubhouse with a large silver bowl beside him," wrote Sharp in the *Chattanooga Times*. "And there was his father, W.G. Oehmig, Jr.— Mr. Bill—and [brothers] Dan Oehmig and Bill Oehmig all around him. Mr. Bill's face was lighted up, too, but it wasn't the sun doing that. He was grinning down to his heart—smiling and happy and proud."

More than 60 years after the fact, Oehmig didn't remember much about his first Tennessee Amateur victory, but he recalled the vanquished Falls with characteristic grace.

"I played pretty well," Oehmig said. "And Ed, he probably had an off day. I just played a little bit better. But Ed was a wonderful guy. We had a good match and enjoyed the day. It was very exciting for a college kid to win the state amateur."

1949—No. 2 Was a Long Time Coming

Though it might have seemed inconceivable to anyone who watched Oehmig win his first Tennessee Amateur in 1937, it took twelve years for him to win another. It wasn't for a lack of trying.

Indeed, Oehmig found himself in the championship match the next year at Jackson Country Club, where he was waxed 8 and 7 by Johnny Cummings, who was perhaps better known for his baseball skills, having

Cary Middlecoff

played for, among several other Class AA teams, the local Chattanooga Lookouts.

"He was a helluva athlete," Oehmig reflected. "He gave me a pretty good beating."

In 1939, the tournament was again played in Oehmig's backyard at Chattanooga Golf and Country Club. Oehmig was qualifying medalist, but H.P. Childress of Memphis won the title, wading through a tough draw that included Riverview club champion Jack Harkins, defending champion Cummings and Ermal Allen, a quarterback for the University of Kentucky, who later served on Tom Landry's staff with the Dallas Cowboys.

Over the next six years, there were two very good reasons Oehmig didn't win the Tennessee Amateur: Cary Middlecoff and World War II.

In 1940, Oehmig, then 24, played 19-year-old Middlecoff in the championship match at Holston Hills Country Club in Knoxville. Middlecoff won 6 and 5.

"I'd never heard of Middlecoff," Oehmig said. "I didn't know anything about him."

Oehmig, and the rest of the golf world, would soon know all about Middlecoff, who etched his name into the game's record books by winning three major championships. Middlecoff, a dentist by trade, was a meticulous (many said slow) player who was plagued throughout his career by physical ailments. But he became one of the greatest players in history. Two skills stood above all others in Middlecoff's game.

"Middlecoff drove the ball farther than most professionals of his day despite his rather short backswing and relatively small degree of shoulder turn," wrote Dick Aultman and Ken Bowden in *The Masters of Golf*. "No doubt his tallness gave him some additional leverage, but it was his precise sense of timing that provided most of his length on full shots. By noticeably pausing at the top of his backswing, he gave his legs and hips ample time to lead all else on his forward swing. This lower-body leadership, when coupled with his steady head position, allowed him to build additional leverage early in his downswing, retain it until near impact, and then fully release it into the ball."

Middlecoff was also a great putter who made some big putts in the clutch. He sank an 82-footer for eagle on the par-5 13th hole at Augusta National to win the 1955 Masters, and made a nerve-wracking four-footer on the final hole of the U.S. Open at Oak Hill Country Club to win that championship.

"As with his full shots, Middlecoff was a perfectionist on the greens in that he tried to hole every putt," wrote Aultman and Bowden in *The Masters of Golf.*

During his reign of terror in the Tennessee Amateur, Middlecoff didn't hole every putt he stood over. But it must have seemed that way to his opponents. He won four straight titles in the early '40s, at Holston Hills in 1940, at Belle Meade in 1941, at Chickasaw Country Club in 1942 and Belle Meade again in 1943. The Army beckoned after that, but after Middlecoff served his tour of duty as a dentist, he headed to the PGA Tour, much to the relief of amateurs in Tennessee.

Oehmig was the first to tangle with Middlecoff in a championship match.

"He hit the ball a country mile," Oehmig said. "He surprised the hell out of me. He got up and down out of traps, from everywhere—he seemed to have a magic touch. He was a nice guy, but cocky as hell. And he beat me like a drum."

Like Middlecoff, Oehmig was also busy during World War II, serving from 1942-1946 in the Naval Reserve, where he served on the *U.S.S. Intrepid* in the Western Pacific. It wasn't until 1948 that his name showed up among the principal characters in an amateur championship. Once again, Oehmig was medalist at his home course. Once again, another player won the title—Wes Brown, who became one of Chattanooga's best amateurs and later operated popular Moccasin Bend Golf Course.

Oehmig finally regained the championship in 1949

in a close match against Jimmy Wittenberg, Sr., of Memphis at Knoxville's Cherokee Country Club. The final 36 holes were plagued by rain, so much so that both players were surprised the match wasn't postponed. The two battled evenly for 36 holes, and neither of them will forget the last one.

The 18th hole at Cherokee is a par-4 with tall trees lining the right side of the fairway.

"I hit my drive right, behind the trees," Oehmig said. "I tried to slice it around there, and it caught a limb and fell down, 80 yards from the green."

"When Lew hit it in the trees, nobody could see it," said Wittenberg, who won the 1947 Tennessee Amateur at Jackson Country Club. "We figured it was out of bounds, but we found it. All Lew could do was knock it out of there and try to get it back to the fairway."

Wittenberg couldn't be blamed for thinking he had the match in his hip pocket, especially after he hit his approach.

"I hit an iron straight at the green," he said. "But it was all uphill, and the ground was wet. My shot came up three feet short of the green and stayed there."

Oehmig, meanwhile, was extricating himself from trouble, hitting a wedge 18 inches from the hole. Wittenberg chipped up to five feet, but couldn't make his par putt.

"And the golfing gods, who had been with the spunky little Memphian all through the round, deserted him," wrote Austin White in the *Chattanooga News-Free Press*. "His second putt, struck firmly, hit the back of the cup, bounded out and hung on the rim as Jimmy's shoulders sagged and the gallery [of more than 1,500] gasped. That was it. A roar, the like of which Knoxville had never seen on a golf course, went up as Oehmig quickly stepped over to congratulate the loser. Their finish was one of the greatest ever staged in a Tennessee golf tournament."

"That was a real thrilling match we had," Oehmig said. "It went back and forth the whole day. I was just lucky enough to win that last hole."

"It took a while for me to come out from under that one," Wittenberg said. "It was hard to believe. But Lew was something. He was quite some player. Tremendous."

Wittenberg never again played in the championship match of the amateur. Twenty-one years later Jimmy Wittenberg, Jr., finished tied for second in the 1970 tournament. The winner? Lew Oehmig.

1951—Another Narrow Victory

Albert Stone, Jr., remembers the first time he ever saw Lew Oehmig play golf. It was 1938, and Oehmig was playing in his second straight Tennessee Amateur against Johnny Cummings at Jackson Country Club.

"I was just 13 years old," Stone said. "I remember pulling for [Lew] but he got beat pretty bad. Not many people beat him after that."

One of the few people to have any sort of mastery over Oehmig in the Tennessee Amateur was Stone, who had a 3-1 match play record against him. Stone, a Jackson native who for years was generally considered the longest player in Tennessee, was a load, even for some of the greatest players in state history.

"There was no player in the state I feared to play in match play more than Albert Stone," Tennessee Golf Hall of Fame member Mason Rudolph said. Stone, who played college golf at Mississippi and briefly considered a career on the PGA Tour (he was talked out of it by good friend Cary Middlecoff), could strike fear in his opponents' hearts with his sheer length. His advantage was the ability to hit short irons into greens when his opponents were hitting mid- and long-irons. Many times, he drove par-4 holes, setting himself up for easy birdies and the occasional eagle.

Stone made golfing history in Tennessee when he won the 1952 Tennessee State Open at his home course, Jackson Country Club, and then two years later won the Tennessee Amateur at Knoxville's Holston Hills. He was the first player to win both championships.

In between those victories, Stone hooked up with Oehmig in the finals of the 1951 Tennessee Amateur. The match was played at Colonial Country Club, where Oehmig had won his first amateur 14 years earlier. It was close throughout.

"The turning point was the 17th hole," Stone said. "I

was 1-up going into 17, which was a par-3. Lew hit the ball way left. I was on the fringe of the green. I'll be dadgum if he didn't hit the most remarkable flop shot for a gimmee. I didn't see how in the world he was going to get it up on the green. I thought that was going to be the match right there."

Stone couldn't get down in two, and the match continued to the par-5 18th. Oehmig won the hole after hitting a fairway wood to the fringe and chipping to two feet. Stone missed a 10-footer for birdie, leaving Oehmig to clean up his short putt for his third Tennessee Amateur.

"When Lew Oehmig puts the trophy emblematic of the 1951 Tennessee Amateur golf championship, which he won yesterday at Colonial Country Club, on the mantelpiece of his Chattanooga home, he ought to stick his wedge in an honored place beside it," wrote Vincent Thillen in the *Memphis Commercial Appeal*.

Oehmig's victory over Stone was his first and last in match play.

"Albert was always a tough competitor for me," Oehmig said. "Over the years we had some great matches, some close matches."

"In four matches, I don't think there was ever more than a hole or two difference," Stone said.

1952—A Home Course Victory at Last

Three times before, Oehmig had played in the Tennessee Amateur at Chattanooga Golf and Country

Club. And three times before, he wasn't able to take advantage of local knowledge and win the championship. His luck changed in 1952.

Oehmig took no prisoners as he finally used his home-course advantage to its fullest. The final match against M.C. James of Knoxville turned into a 6 and 5 route.

The *Chattanooga Times* noted Oehmig's dominance for a week of golf at the Riverview course.

"The 6,305-yard par-70 course held few fears for him from first round to last," wrote George Short. "He was under par in a warmup round [65], scored a 67 in pro-amateur competition and closed out all his foes on the 17th hole or before."

In the final match that lasted just 31 holes, Oehmig beat James into submission early with a 4-under-par 66 in the morning round. That included an eagle at the par-5 7th hole as he drained a 20-foot putt. Oehmig didn't play as well in the afternoon match, but managed a second eagle when he holed a 130-yard second shot at the par-4 10th hole.

"I'd known M.C. all my life and he was a good friend," Oehmig said. "We'd played in a lot of tournaments together. I hated that the match was so one-sided, but it was one of those days I happened to be on and he was off."

Oehmig's victory was his third in four years and the fifth straight for a Chattanoogan. Wes Brown won the title in 1948, and Billy Ragland in 1950.

The win placed Oehmig in some fast company. His fourth championship tied him for second-place all-time with two great players, Cary Middlecoff, who by this time was winning major championships on the PGA Tour, and Polly Boyd of Chattanooga. Emmett Spicer of Memphis held the record of five championships. It took Oehmig another three years to catch him.

1955—Beating a Youngster

Just as a young Lew Oehmig was intimidated by Spicer in the 1934 Tennessee Amateur, Oehmig would later go on to intimidate younger opponents through the years. One of those youngsters was 20-year-old Ed Brantly, who became one of the best amateurs in Chattanooga, Tennessee, and the U.S.

In the summer of 1955, Brantly, a Signal Mountain native who played two years of college golf at Tennessee, was in the process of transferring to the University of Memphis (then known as Memphis State). Before heading West, Brantly hooked up with Oehmig in the Tennessee Amateur finals at Nashville's Belle Meade. The results weren't pretty. Oehmig won the 36-hole match, 10 and 8, as he tied Spicer's record of five career championships.

"If life begins at 40, as some optimistic, rejuvenated gent once quipped, the rest of Tennessee's amateur golfers are facing a bleak future because 39-year-old Lew Oehmig is approaching that milepost and is showing darn few signs of yielding to the ravages of old man time," wrote Austin White in the *Chattanooga News-Free Press* after Oehmig's victory.

Brantly remembers well his match with the veteran Oehmig.

"That was one of the first times I'd ever played him," Brantly said. "I was fairly young, and he really intimidated me."

Oehmig was trying to win his fourth Tennessee Amateur in a seven-year stretch and also make a little bit of history by tying Spicer with five career championships. "I didn't have much sympathy in my heart, I'm sure," Oehmig said of playing the youthful Brantly.

The match got off to an ominous start for Brantly, who double-bogeyed the par-4 third hole to go 1 down.

"It didn't get much better after that," Brantly said.

Try as he might, Brantly couldn't make much headway against Oehmig. On the par-5 8th hole in the morning round, Brantly was just short of the green in two. Oehmig was over the green and in a bunker in three.

"I chipped it up close for birdie and I'm thinking I'm going to win the hole," Brantly said. "Then he goes and chips it in. I didn't lose the hole, but I didn't win the hole, either."

Oehmig led 1-up after the first nine, then made five birdies in a six-hole span en route to a 33 on the back

to Brantly's 38. That increased his lead to 5-up heading into the afternoon round, which ended when
Oehmig won the par-3 10th.

Oehmig remembers being on top of his game against
Brantly.

"Everything I hit went in the hole that day," Oehmig
said. "It was just one of those days when the good
Lord smiles on you."

After the drubbing, Brantly resolved to elevate his
game.

"I took away the fact that, if I'm going to beat him,
I'm going to have to play better," Brantly said.

And play better Brantly did. He went on to an excel-
lent amateur career and even briefly considered play-
ing the PGA Tour. In 1957, Brantly won the first of
three Tennessee Amateurs with a 4 and 2 victory over
Gene Frase of Memphis at Chattanooga Golf and
Country Club. That same summer, he also won the
Southern Amateur, becoming only the third
Chattanoogan to play in the finals of that tournament
(A.W. Grimes and Ewing Watkins were the others)
and only the second to win it (Grimes won in 1903).

In 1958, Brantly enlisted in the Air Force, and he
continued to play great golf while stationed in Europe.
Brantly was low amateur in the 1959 and 1960
German Opens and won the 1959 German Amateur.

Returning to the U.S. in 1961, Brantly qualified for
that year's U.S. Open—becoming the first
Chattanoogan to do so—and made the cut at Oakland

Hills along with fellow amateurs Jack Nicklaus and Deane Beman. Brantly also qualified for the 1962 Open at Oakmont, but missed the cut.

Closer to home, Brantly won his second Tennessee Amateur in 1961 with a 1-up victory over Albert Stone, Jr., at Colonial. Always known as a great putter, Brantly one-putted five of the last six holes to beat Stone.

It took 17 years, but Brantly finally got the best of Oehmig in the Tennessee Amateur, beating him in 1972 at Lookout Mountain Golf Club, which had become Oehmig's home course. That was Brantly's last amateur title, but he went on to win three Tennessee Senior Amateurs.

"I had a great relationship with Lew," Brantly said. "I've always admired him. I'll never forget when I was younger I always used to call him Mr. Oehmig. Mr. Oehmig this. Mr. Oehmig that. I can't remember what year it was, but he looked at me one time and said, 'My name is Lew. You call me Lew from now on.' I said, 'Yes, sir, Mr. Oehmig.' "

Oehmig had similar respect for Brantly. At a Baylor School homecoming luncheon in October 2000, the two old adversaries saw one another for the first time in years.

"Eddie always used to beat me like a stick," Oehmig told one of his grandchildren.

"Yeah, maybe with one arm tied behind your back," Brantly said.

1962—Beating a Youngster, Part II

During a career that spanned five decades, Oehmig played every good rising amateur in Tennessee. In 1962, he had to beat one of the best players the state had produced to that point, Bobby Greenwood of Cookeville. That year, Greenwood wasn't just one of Tennessee's finest players. He was ranked among the top 10 amateurs nationally, and was in the middle of an excellent college career at North Texas State, where he was a three-time All-American.

In those days, Greenwood was a dominant player. He remembers fondly one summer when he won 13 tournaments—"most of them were those little, one-day fried chickens," he said—but Greenwood didn't just pick on the little guys. In the 1961 Colonial Amateur Invitational in Memphis, he beat Jack Nicklaus, who had won his second U.S. Amateur that year, with a birdie-eagle-birdie finish. A year later, Nicklaus, then a PGA Tour rookie, won the U.S. Open.

In the early-to-mid-'60s, Greenwood fashioned a great stretch of golf during which he played in the Tennessee Amateur finals three times from 1962-1966. Three years after Greenwood won his second amateur, at Chickasaw Country Club, he joined the PGA Tour, where he played for seven seasons.

As good as he was, Greenwood remembers feeling intimidated when he squared off against the great Oehmig in the 1962 amateur finals on Oehmig's home turf, Chattanooga Golf and Country Club.

Lew Oehmig reacts to a putt during his 1962 Tennessee Amateur victory at Chattanooga Golf and Country Club

Oehmig had long been a hero of Greenwood's.

"Growing up, Lew Oehmig was a great inspiration to me," Greenwood said. "Because he was different than most players in that he had such class and dignity. He dressed beautifully, looked good and acted gracious. He was a real, true gentleman. I've played matches against Byron Nelson and Jack Nicklaus, and they didn't come into the same class as far as the warmth Lew showed to me as a young man trying to learn to play the game."

Greenwood will never forget his match against Oehmig. He led most of the way.

"Which was interesting," Greenwood said. "When you're 1- or 2-up on somebody, you can see their demeanor, how they act toward you. Lew was nice to me and a real gentleman the entire match."

Oehmig, as he often did in the state amateur, rallied and eventually tied Greenwood at the end of 36 holes. That forced a playoff, which started at the par-4 first hole.

"I remember really having mixed emotions at the time," Greenwood said. "Lew was on his home course. He had so many fans watching him play; they all seemed to love him. And here I was, the young guy trying to knock off the great Lew Oehmig."

The playoff didn't last long. Oehmig's drive split the fairway, but Greenwood drove into the left rough. Greenwood had to hit his approach over the bunker that guarded the left of the green, but it fell short and buried in the sand. Oehmig hit his approach to 30 feet.

"When I walked down to the bunker, I saw I had a buried lie," Greenwood said. "I said, 'This match is over.'"

Greenwood was right. For the second time, Oehmig had won Tennessee golf's most coveted championship on his boyhood course.

"It was a wonderful match, very exciting," Oehmig said. "I remember thinking that Bobby was a fine golfer. I was sure he'd play on the tour someday."

When Greenwood first played Oehmig, he admittedly didn't think he could win. That changed the next time the two played.

"It was four years later [at the 1966 amateur at Chickasaw]," Greenwood said. "I finally had enough confidence to think I was the best player in Tennessee. We played an early-round match, and we both parred the first hole. In the second fairway, Lew said, 'Bobby, take it easy on the old man today.' He was about 10 yards behind me. I stopped, and waited for him to come up.

"I said, 'Lew, I'm gonna beat you as bad as I can beat you.' And Lew looked at me like, you've arrived. You've got the game."

Greenwood did beat Oehmig, but the match was close. He later defeated Bob Lundy of Memphis for the championship.

"I'll never forget that last match we played," Greenwood said. "He was a good sport as a winner, and also in defeat. What more can you say about a man than that?"

1970—Winning at Stroke Play

Despite the fact that he had won six Tennessee Amateurs at match play, Oehmig was long a proponent of stroke play to determine a significant championship. As a three-time president of the Tennessee Golf Association and a member of its board of directors for more than 40 years, he was in a position to make his opinion known.

"I'll never forget 1967," Oehmig said. "It was a big controversy among the board as to whether or not we should go to medal play. I was always in favor of medal play, because I thought it produced the better champion. In match play, you could have one bad round and be out of the tournament. In four days of stroke play, you could survive a bad round. I'd seen plenty of good players get knocked out in the first round in match play."

The TGA had a tough time with the decision. The amateur was played at stroke play in 1967, returned to match in 1968, reverted to medal play in 1969 and has stayed that way ever since.

It was only fitting that Oehmig was a principal character in the tournament's first try at stroke play, in 1967 at Chattanooga Golf and Country Club. He was tied for the lead after 63 holes with Chattanoogans Ed Brantly and Larry White, the city's newest young star.

White was then a junior at the University of Houston, where he played for the legendary Dave Williams. In White's time at Houston, the Cougars won three NCAA championships.

White was understandably a bit nervous at the prospect of playing a nine-hole duel for the championship with Oehmig and Brantly, who by this time had won eight Tennessee Amateurs between them. "I knew I'd have to beat Lew and Brantly if I wanted to win the tournament," White said. "It was Lew's home course, and Ed was one of the best players in the state."

White took the fight to the two veterans, shooting 31 on the back nine and winning his first amateur by four shots over Oehmig.

It was a crucial two-stroke swing on the 14th hole that turned the match in White's favor. White drained a 20-foot putt for a birdie, and Oehmig missed a four-footer for par.

"He didn't lose it," said White, who went on to play the PGA Tour. "I just went out and won it. I was scared to death. I just happened to play the last nine holes really well and made some long putts."

Stroke play and the advancing years did nothing to diminish Oehmig's competitiveness in the Tennessee Amateur. He was a contender for many years to come. Oehmig finished fourth in 1969, and in 1970, at 54, won his seventh championship while beating several players 20 to 30 years his junior.

That tournament, played at Nashville's Richland

Country Club, was no contest through 54 holes. Oehmig opened with rounds of 69-68-72 at the par-71 course and led by seven shots heading into the last day. But the final round was plagued by rain, and Oehmig shot a 4-over-par 40 on the front nine, allowing several players to creep back into the tournament. At the 14th hole, Oehmig led by just one over Chattanooga's Ed Brantly and Jimmy Wittenberg, Jr., and by two over Memphis State student Randy Hudson.

It turned out Oehmig had his pursuers right where he wanted them. At the par-3 14th, Oehmig saved par from the back bunker while the other three contenders made bogeys. He holed a breaking, six-foot par putt at No. 15, then finished par-birdie-par for a final round 77 and a 2-over-par 284 for the tournament, four shots clear of Mike Buja, Wittenberg and Hudson.

"Those boys were good to me today," Oehmig told the *Nashville Tennessean* after the round. "If any of them had shot 70 it would have been a tie ball game. I kept reading and hearing how easy today was going to be, and I must have believed it."

A few weeks later, Oehmig won his second straight Tennessee Senior Amateur at Deane Hill in Knoxville, making him the first (and so far only) player to win the state amateur and senior amateur titles in the same year. Dick Horton, executive director of the Tennessee Golf Association, thinks it will be hard for anyone to duplicate that feat.

"You never say never," Horton said. "But I highly doubt a senior can ever again win both the amateur and senior amateur titles in the same year. With the senior amateur age at 55, and amateur golf so strong in Tennessee—with excellent college golfers and junior players and great mid-amateurs like Danny Green and Tim Jackson—I just don't see it. Your best chance might be with a Green or Jackson, but it's hard to imagine it."

1971—Number Eight Leaves Lasting Legacy

It was fitting that in the last Tennessee Amateur that Oehmig won, he established a record that has yet to be broken. At 55 years old, Oehmig shot 282 for four rounds at Colonial Country Club, beating runner-up Ronnie Wenzler of Memphis by seven shots. That's the largest margin of victory since the tournament switched to a medal play format in 1967.

Oehmig's victory was as easy as it seemed. He shot even par for three rounds, carding three straight 70s.

"I guess I'm hung up on 70," Oehmig told the *Memphis Commercial-Appeal.* "How does a guy go about getting out of a rut like this?"

Oehmig broke out of that rut with a final round 72, but though he finally shot over par, no one could catch him.

"Oh, I just dogged it around," Oehmig said after the round. "These kids just decided to be kind to us old folks. It seems like just yesterday that I started playing this game, but I guess it was a little longer than that."

Oehmig drew considerable praise from the youngsters he defeated at Colonial.

"He's a great player," Wenzler said. "That's all you can say."

"That Mr. Oehmig, he's something else," said 19-year-old chip Rockholt, who finished tied for fourth and would win his own state amateur seven years later at Jackson Country Club. "He keeps it in play, and that's what you've gotta do. When you play him, you just can't make a mistake of any kind. He's just super."

Only four other players in state history have won as many as three state amateurs. Emmett Spicer of Memphis won five before moving out of the state. Chattanooga's Polly Boyd won four, as did Cary Middlecoff, who turned pro in 1946. Ed Brantly of Chattanooga won three times.

"At 55, Lew Oehmig of Chattanooga is the greatest," wrote long-time *Nashville Banner* golf writer Dudley "Waxo" Green, who would one day join Oehmig in the Tennessee Golf Hall of Fame. "He just keeps rolling along, winning the Tennessee Amateur with a style that borders on classic."

Oehmig added to his 1971 accomplishments by pulling another double, winning the Tennessee Senior Amateur for the third straight time at Rivermont Golf Club in Chattanooga.

Three that got away

As many Tennessee Amateurs as Oehmig won, there were probably as many more he could have won. Three near misses particularly haunted him.

The first was in 1951 at Nashville's old Richland Country Club (the club has since relocated to a Jack Nicklaus-designed layout). Oehmig, who led most of the match, lost to young Chattanoogan Billy Ragland, 1-up. Ragland played for Princeton, where he competed in several NCAA championships and the U.S. Amateur.

"Winning the Tennessee Amateur meant a lot to me," said Ragland, who at 69 could still shoot his age at The Honors Course in 2000. "I had a lot of family in Nashville. We had a big celebration afterward."

"That was one match I really regret losing," Oehmig said. "I had him down most of the time. I don't remember which holes he won toward the end. I remember the last hole. I knew I had to win it. I missed a lot of putts. That's one of those I tried to forget."

Ragland had an unusual strategy for staying in the match with Oehmig.

"I don't think I was old enough to realize how good he was," Ragland said.

Then again, perhaps he was. Whenever it was Oehmig's turn to hit, Ragland turned his back on him.

"I looked away when he swung," Ragland said. "He had such a beautiful swing, so rhythmic. It was almost hypnotic."

Mason Rudolph

A stint in the Navy served to effectively end Ragland's promising tournament career, but he later qualified for two U.S. Senior Opens, once playing with Arnold Palmer.

Just like the great Palmer, Oehmig experienced a monumental collapse in a significant championship. Palmer lost a seven-shot lead with eight holes to play in the 1966 U.S. Open and handed the tournament to Billy Casper. Ten years before that in the 1956 Tennessee Amateur, Oehmig led young Mason Rudolph 7-up with nine holes to play at Chickasaw in Memphis and still lost.

Rudolph, a native of Clarksville, wasn't an ordinary player. In 1950, he won the U.S. Junior Amateur, and also qualified for the U.S. Open at Merion. He's still the youngest Open qualifier at 16 years, 15 days. Rudolph also qualified for the Open in 1951.

Along with his state amateur title, Rudolph won the Tennessee Open in 1956, so it isn't a stretch to suggest he was playing the best golf of anybody in the state at that time. He later turned pro, won five more state opens and enjoyed a solid career on the PGA Tour. In

1991, Rudolph was one of seven charter inductees into the Tennessee Golf Hall of Fame.

In 2000, *Golf World* magazine chose Rudolph the 10th-best junior of the 20th century, which placed him in the strongest of company—Tiger Woods, Jack Nicklaus, Bobby Jones and Phil Mickelson were also in the top 10.

Rudolph remembers well the final holes of his great comeback against Oehmig. The oppressive heat of Memphis in August is particularly etched in Rudolph's memory.

"It must have been 105 degrees," he said.

Oehmig led 3-up with three holes to play, but Rudolph won the difficult par-4 16th hole with a par and the short par-4 17th with a birdie. Oehmig still led 1-up heading into the home hole.

"The 18th hole was very tight," Rudolph said. "There were trees left and right. Lew hit his tee shot in the trees and didn't get his ball on the green until his third shot. I won that hole with a par."

That sent the match to extra holes. Oehmig got into trouble again, and after three shots, he was still 20 feet from the hole. Rudolph was on the fringe in two. With a 3-iron, he rolled the ball into the hole for the victory.

"That was the biggest comeback I can ever remember," Rudolph said. "The odds on beating Lew were high. He was a premier player in the state. I was fortunate to come back like that. In golf, that can happen, when the wheels start falling off."

"It was one of those things where I'd make par and he's make birdie," Oehmig said. "And if I'd make bogey, he'd make par."

Oehmig and Rudolph formed a bond that day.

"Mason's a wonderful guy," Oehmig said. "He's always been a good friend."

"I always admired Lew Oehmig," Rudolph said. "He's a tough competitor but a true gentleman."

Oehmig's last near miss came when he was 56 years old. It was 1972, and by this time the amateur was firmly entrenched as a stroke-play tournament. The venue was Lookout Mountain, which Oehmig had joined many years before after his family moved from Riverview to the mountain.

The tournament wound down to another duel between Oehmig, who was seeking to win his third straight title, and Ed Brantly, who had made a name for himself playing out of Chattanooga's other mountain course, Signal Mountain. Oehmig was trying to win his ninth Tennessee amateur, Brantly his third.

On the final hole of the tournament, Oehmig trailed Brantly by a stroke. The 18th at Lookout Mountain is a short par 4, but out of bounds looms large to the right and trees to the left.

"I told myself I wasn't going to hit the ball right," Brantly said. "So consequently, I hit it left into the trees."

Oehmig, never one to back off, stepped up to the tee

with a driver and drove his ball out of bounds. He wound up with a double-bogey on the hole to Brantly's bogey. Brantly finished the tournament in 285 strokes, Oehmig 287.

Oehmig's time as a contender in the tournament he'd dominated for years wasn't quite over. Eight years later, at 64, Oehmig was only four shots out of the lead after three rounds at Colonial Country Club, where he had won his first Tennessee Amateur 43 years before.

"I feel like I'm right in there," Oehmig told the *Chattanooga News-Free Press.* "If I'm two or three under tomorrow, I could win."

Oehmig was 1-under par for the first seven holes in the final round, but the tough par-4 8th hole derailed him. Oehmig made a double-bogey there, also had a double at No. 10, and triple-bogeyed 13. He finished with a 78 and tied for seventh.

Oehmig never again appeared on a Tennessee Amateur leaderboard, but he stayed active in TGA events, winning senior amateurs at Brentwood in 1982 and Stones River in 1983. Like his record in the state amateur, Oehmig's senior amateur accomplishments aren't likely to be equaled.

He won five straight from 1969 to 1973 and wound up with a total of seven championships. No other player has won more than three titles.

No one recalls why the TGA didn't play the senior amateur from 1974 to 1979, but some have speculated that Oehmig's dominance kept the field so low the tournament wasn't worth conducting. When the senior amateur returned in 1980, Oehmig was still around. He finished second at his home course, Lookout Mountain, to old friend Ira Templeton that year, and second to Templeton again in 1981. Oehmig put the capper to a long and successful Tennessee amateur golf career with his final two senior victories in 1982 and 1983.

In his career, the only significant state title that eluded Oehmig was the Tennessee Open. He came close during a three-year stretch in the early '50s, finishing third as Templeton won in 1951 at Signal Mountain; second to Albert Stone, Jr., the next year when the tournament was played at Stone's home course in Jackson; and third to fellow Tennessee Golf Hall of Fame member Curtis Person, Sr., at Richland in 1952.

Twenty-nine years after his final Tennessee Amateur victory and 19 after his last win in the senior amateur, the exploits of Lew Oehmig still inspired the state's best players.

"When you get past your mid-60s, it's hard to win," 64-year-old Marty Graham told the *Memphis Commerical Appeal* after winning his second Tennessee Senior Amateur at Ridgeway Country Club in the summer of 2000. "But ol' Lew Oehmig is my idol. He won his third U.S. Senior Amateur at 69. I'm not comparing myself with him because he's such a super-great player, but knowing he did it is an inspiration to me."

Oehmig, who didn't regularly play national amateur events until his mid-50s because of business and family obligations, chose instead to support his home state's golf association and tournaments. Though his record in Tennessee golf was gratifying to him, Oehmig, as he did throughout his life, downplayed his accomplishments.

"If you think about it, during the almost 40-year period during which those tournaments were won, a lot of the great amateurs in the state turned pro," Oehmig said. "I'm not sure I could have won as many if people like Cary Middlecoff and Mason Rudolph had remained amateurs. But there was still a lot of competition. It was no cakewalk.

"It was all a wonderful experience that I wouldn't take anything for. It was very gratifying. I had a lot of support from my family, friends; even the boys in the press were good to me.

"Tennessee golf was a big part of my life. My dad got me started at an early age, and I was fortunate enough to stay competitive for a number of years. I'm not sure why that was, except to say that it's just built into you; the will to win. Some people have that, and some people don't."

CHAPTER 4

LEW AND IRA

"I asked Ira what was so special about being the first amateur to ever win the Tennessee State Open, and his reply was classic: 'The thing that was so special about the Open championship is that Oehmig never won it.' Of all the state titles that Lew claimed, the Open eluded him and Ira just loved the fact that he could needle his buddy one more time!"

—Dick Horton

A ll throughout golf's modern era, great players have thrived by virtue of having a rival—other excellent players who have provided them with competition and pushed them to succeed. Ben Hogan had Sam Snead and Byron Nelson. Arnold Palmer had Jack Nicklaus. Nicklaus had Lee Trevino, Johnny Miller and Tom Watson. Tiger Woods has … well, perhaps there is an exception to every rule.

For much of his adult playing career, Lew Oehmig had the perfect foil, a player whose style and demeanor were in direct contrast to his own, but whose golfing skills, particularly on the greens, offered the very challenge for which Oehmig played

Ira Templeton, Jr.

the game.

Ira Franklin Templeton, Jr., was born in Chattanooga on Nov. 29, 1924, and though he grew up in close proximity to Oehmig, it wasn't until later in life that the two men became inseparable companions on the golf course. Templeton was closer in age to Oehmig's brother Dan, and would occasionally spend the night at the Oehmigs' home on 1416 Winding Way in Riverview. Like Lew, Templeton was a member at Chattanooga Golf and Country Club and played for the Baylor School golf team. But because Oehmig was eight years older, the two had little interaction.

"I really didn't know Ira back then," Oehmig said. "I was 16, 17, 18 years old, and he was quite a bit younger. He knew my brothers [Dan and Bill]. I was so far ahead of him in school. We didn't have reason to spend time with one another."

At that stage of their lives, Oehmig and Templeton didn't have much in common. Oehmig graduated with honors from Baylor and later studied law at the University of Virginia. Templeton transferred from Baylor to Central because the academic load at Baylor was too tough. Oehmig played for Baylor's golf team from the seventh grade on; Templeton was never more than fifth man for Baylor or Central.

Templeton—though he was introduced to the game at an early age and, like Oehmig, schooled by Wilbur Oakes, the old Scottish pro at Chattanooga Golf and Country Club—had more pressing concerns in high

Lew Oehmig with Ira Templeton.

school. At 16, he met a Central student named Dorothy Wallace and was smitten; the two, married in 1944, would spend the rest of their lives together. And Templeton, though painfully thin, loved football. He was a tailback on a great Central team that was 11-1 and finished second in the state in 1942.

One day after he graduated from Central in May 1943, Templeton joined the Air Force. He was trained as a pilot for a year, but his tour of duty in World War II was viewed from a different vantage point than the air.

"I washed out of pilot training," Templeton said. "So I went to radio school. I was a ground operator. I was at sea when they dropped the first atomic bomb. The cheers on that boat were unbelievable, because all of us knew what we were in for had the war not ended. We were hoping the boat would turn around right then."

Templeton returned home in March 1945. Three months later, his father, Ira, Sr., died of a heart attack. He was 44.

"He was an alcoholic," Templeton said. "Overweight. He didn't take care of himself. But he had a good business."

The senior Templeton's business was a jewelry store. But even though he was set up with a career, Templeton wasn't interested.

"Ira just wasn't cut out to stay behind the counter and run a jewelry store," Oehmig said.

Templeton admitted as much.

"I never did any good with the jewelry store, because I was always at the country club," Templeton said.

After the war, golf began to get its hooks into Templeton. In 1947, he took in his first Masters Tournament. The trip to Augusta inspired him.

"I guess it was about 1947, '48, I got the bug," Templeton said. "I really did. I just ate, drank and slept golf. That's all I thought about."

Templeton did have to make a living, though, and he tried a variety of businesses. He opened a brake shop for a time, and also dabbled in the vending machine business. He sold cars and later golf equipment for Chattanooga-based First Flight (where Oehmig, then the company's president, was his boss). Templeton eventually discovered his life's calling when he took over the management of Eastgate Golf Center in 1967. Eight years later, in partnership with Oehmig, Gene Abercrombie and Julius Chazen, he bought Creeks Bend Golf Club, and would spend the rest of his life running the club, buying it outright in 1988.

In between his various business endeavors, the former fifth man on Baylor's golf team was turning himself into an excellent player. And that began to attract the attention of Oehmig.

In 1949, Templeton was a brash 25-year-old, and the 33-year-old Oehmig had already established himself as one of Tennessee's most formidable players, having won two state amateurs and four Chattanooga Metro Amateurs by then.

"Ira set a spark off in me," Oehmig said. "He was always so full of confidence and conversation. You just couldn't help but be attracted to the guy. For years, I hadn't paid much attention to him, and then he came along as a strong young golfer with all the confidence in the world."

Templeton didn't mind sharing his confidence.

"He was as cocky as he could be," Oehmig said. "That's how he got his nickname. As a young guy, Ira was rather lippy, to older people or anyone. One day old Jack Harkins [the boisterous Chattanooga Golf and Country Club member and founder of the Professional Golf Company] looked at him and said, 'Ira, you remind me of a young bird. All mouth and no ass.' Ira was skinny as hell back then. So the name stuck. Young Bird."

The name was later shortened to just "Bird," and Templeton would carry it with him the rest of his life. Beginning in the late '40s, Bird and the man known by sports writers as "Sweet Swinging Lew" became constant companions on the golf course, battling one another in friendly dog fights at the country club, in local and statewide tournaments, and, later in life, on the senior amateur circuit.

It was a few years after getting serious about the game that Templeton made his presence known on the state and local scene. The year was 1951, and Templeton enjoyed a breakout season, winning the Tennessee Open and two other local tournaments, including the Brainerd Invitational. Templeton was the first amateur in Tennessee Open history to win the championship. The victory paved the way for many more to come.

The state open was played in Templeton's back yard in 1951, at Signal Mountain Golf and Country Club. Though much more familiar with the Riverview layout, Templeton seemed at home at Signal, shooting a pair of 67s in a 36-hole finale. His winning total of 9-under-par 207 was a record that stood for 14 years.

Templeton beat Memphis professional Pat Abbott by two shots. Oehmig was third at 211. Templeton's victory was a popular one.

"Ira Templeton's victory in the State Open was well received by all golfers here," said a story in the *Chattanooga News-Free Press*. "There was something about [it] that hit a particularly responsive chord—everyone liked Ira, and he had never before won a tournament. ...

"...What had Ira won in golf before the state victory? 'Nothing,' said the 26-year-old champ. 'I have been playing since I was 10 years old. Dad put me in the TVI meet here 15 years ago. In recent years, I have been a fair golfer, but two months ago I suddenly started playing better. The secret of golf is playing lots ... practice, practice. The only man who can step out on the course without practice and give you a good round is Lew Oehmig. He's a wonder.' "

Surprisingly, Templeton never won another statewide tournament until he was a senior (he won the Tennessee Senior Amateur in 1979 and 1980.) But he was a scourge in Chattanooga golf circles for years, winning numerous tournaments. Templeton didn't let up on the youngsters even after he began competing in senior tournaments. In 1986, Templeton won the Chattanooga Men's Metro—at 61.

This isn't to suggest Templeton wasn't competitive in state tournaments when he was in his prime. He finished second to Jerry Sayres in the 1964 Tennessee

Amateur at Knoxville's Holston Hills and second among amateurs in the 1954 state open won by Abbott at Nashville's Belle Meade Country Club.

Though Templeton never met Oehmig in a championship match, he hooked up with his old friend in some memorable duels in the Tennessee Amateur.

In 1951 at Colonial Country Club in Memphis, Templeton drew Oehmig in the quarterfinals, shot 4-over-par on the front nine and found himself 4 down. He played the next seven holes in 4 under par, but won just one hole—either Templeton or Oehmig made a birdie for seven straight holes.

"A guy who was following us came up later and said it was the damndest golf he'd ever seen," Templeton said. Oehmig beat Templeton 3 and 2 and eventually won the championship, the third of his career.

Templeton and Oehmig provided some more excitement in the 1953 amateur at Jackson Country Club. The duo came to the last hole with Templeton holding a 1-up lead. Things looked good for Templeton after Oehmig faded his tee shot at the par-4 into the rough. From that position, Oehmig lashed his approach onto the green, but 42 feet away from the hole. Templeton nestled his approach to within 10 feet.

A crowd had gathered around the 18th green, as an upset of the man who had won three of the last four state amateurs appeared imminent. Templeton seized the moment.

"I was kidding him as we walked up the fairway,"

Templeton said. "We'd driven to Memphis together, but I told him, 'You know, there's a bus that leaves here about 6 o'clock. If you don't mind, you can catch that 7 o'clock flight out of Memphis and leave the car here with me.' "

"He didn't lend me much sympathy," Oehmig said.

As it turned out, Oehmig didn't need any sympathy.

"His putt was coming down the hill," Templeton said. "It hit the back of the cup and must have bounced a foot high. I can still see it as it went in. I hit a good putt that hung on the lip. I waited for a few seconds, but it didn't fall."

The match went to extra holes. On the third hole, Oehmig drained a 30-foot birdie putt to win. He couldn't resist needling Templeton.

"I told old Bird he'd better start looking for that Greyhound bus," Oehmig said. "They had a place on there reserved for him."

Over the years, Templeton—sometimes with Oehmig and sometimes without him—got to test his game against high-level competition. He played in a PGA Tour event, the 1955 Phoenix Open. There were exhibitions against Arnold Palmer, Bobby Locke and Tommy Bolt. The match against Palmer, played in Virginia, was the soon-to-be-King's first professional event. Templeton shot 67, and Palmer, fresh from his victory in the 1954 U.S. Amateur, 68.

Beating the man who popularized golf for the masses was a career highlight for Templeton, but the exhibition that stood out in his mind came in 1951. In that event, Templeton teamed with Oehmig against Georgia amateur Hobart Manley and the great Ben Hogan.

Hogan had just made golf history by winning consecutive U.S. Open championships. He'd won the 1950 Open at Merion, and defended his title at Oakland Hills–the "monster," as Hogan so famously put it, that he brought to its knees with a final-round 67.

In those days, with purses on the PGA Tour so small, even the highest level professionals had to earn extra cash playing exhibition matches. Hogan set a torrid pace in the summer of 1951, playing in 22 exhibitions. His stop at Chattanooga Golf and Country Club was preceded in the same week by exhibitions at Cincinnati, Lexington, Ky., and Jackson, Tenn.; after Chattanooga, he would head to Birmingham, Ala.

Nearly 50 years later, golfers in Chattanooga still talk about Hogan's appearance. More than 3,000 fans showed up, but it seems as though ten times that many claim to have been there. Some have foggy memories of the great event—Hogan and Manley won, 1-up, but many people think Templeton and Oehmig were the victors.

Though Oehmig could manage only a 6-over-par 76 on his home course and Templeton shot 73, the match came down to the last hole. Manley's par 3 at 18 was enough to win the hole and the match after Oehmig and Templeton missed six- to eight foot par putts.

Hogan, who struggled with a pulled ligament in his right hand suffered in an exhibition two days before in Jackson, shot 72. Manley finished at 73.

Many details of the match have escaped Oehmig and Templeton through the years, but neither will forget their day in the sun with Hogan.

"You couldn't believe the people that were there," Templeton said. "I'll never forget on the old No. 2 tee, I stood up there and there were people lining both sides. I looked at Hogan and said, 'Mr. Hogan, you might be able to hit that ball through there, but I foul it too many times.' He said, 'What side do you want them off of?' I always play a fade, so I told him the left side. And he got them off."

Oehmig and Templeton have different recollections of Hogan, whose steely, taciturn on-course demeanor was legendary.

"Hogan was very friendly," Templeton said. "When I read the things that I read about Hogan, I almost question them. He was so friendly. I asked him one thing about golf that day, something about my grip. He told me to hold it more in the fingers of my left hand. And I did it."

Oehmig still remembers a comment Manley made about riding in a golf cart all day with Bantam Ben.

"Hobart told me later, 'You know, that whole round Hogan never spoke to me, never said a damn thing, until the 17th hole,' " Oehmig said. "I couldn't believe

From left to right: Ben Hogan, Hobart Manley,
Ira Templeton and Lew Oehmig in 1952

it. Hobart was a very outgoing guy with lots of personality. I just couldn't imagine 17 holes without a
word between them."

But that wasn't Oehmig's last impression of Hogan.

"He warmed up after that," Oehmig said. "We saw
him a number of times at Augusta. I remember having
breakfast with him at the same place we stayed. We
had some very pleasant conversations together. He
was human after all."

Not all of Oehmig and Templeton's high-stakes
matches were as well publicized as the one they
played against Hogan and Manley. Templeton always

loved to play for a little cash. Oehmig did occasionally, but most people who knew the two of them wouldn't think about letting them partner in a money game.

Templeton remembers well an exception to that rule.

"I'd gone over and played in the [1957] North Georgia Invitational [in Dalton]," Templeton said. "When it was over, Doug Sanders came up to me and said to get Lew and we'd play in Chattanooga on Monday."

This was two weeks before Sanders, a native of Cedartown, Ga., would turn pro. Sanders, who won the 1956 Canadian Open as an amateur, went on to a long and successful career on the PGA Tour, where he won 20 tournaments and gained notoriety for his flamboyant style and flashy dress. Sanders later played the Senior Tour. Well before he started playing for pay officially, Sanders liked to wager a little. He brought a player from Dalton with him to take on Oehmig and Templeton.

"He called me the next morning," Templeton said. "I told him I got Lew. We thought we were going to play at the [Chattanooga] country club. But he wanted to go to Signal Mountain."

Sanders' reasoning for wanting to play at Signal Mountain is unclear. Perhaps Sanders, who would later write a book, *130 Different Ways to Make a Bet*, didn't know Templeton had won the Tennessee Open and Oehmig finished third at Signal in 1951.

Templeton and Oehmig can't remember what the bet

was that day, but it was for a lot more than Templeton usually wagered ("My standard bet was a $10 nassau," he said). After they shot a best-ball score of 13 under par, Oehmig and Templeton lined their pockets as Sanders retreated to Georgia.

"I didn't hear any more from him for a while," Templeton said. "Doug was trying to hustle. That's the part Lew and I enjoyed. Doug was a helluva player. We didn't have any business playing him. He just went to the wrong golf course. I was such a good putter, and Lew was a great wedge player. We putted for a lot of birdies up there."

That wasn't the last Templeton and Oehmig saw of Sanders, who later played First Flight equipment and came to Chattanooga often.

"Doug and I were friends," Templeton said. "He'd come to Chattanooga and he'd always call."

"It was a pleasure to match your game against someone like Lew or Ira," Sanders said. "The thing I found out about them real quick was that they hated to lose. They both had that killer instinct. When you played those guys, you'd better have had your 'A' game or you were gonna walk away afterward with your wallet a lot lighter."

Oehmig and Templeton didn't get to play as partners very often, but they regularly played in the same tournaments through the years, continuing their strong play well into their senior careers. Oehmig became the only three-time winner of the U.S. Senior Amateur and won a record seven Tennessee Senior Amateurs. Templeton won the Tennessee Senior Amateur twice and won the Legendary Senior Amateur in what was his biggest victory on the national scene. In one four-year stretch—from 1979 through 1982—the state senior amateur was won by either Templeton (1979, 1980) or Oehmig (1981, 1982).

Templeton never did break through in the U.S. Senior Amateur, but a near miss in that tournament haunted him for months afterward. It was 1985, and the venue was Wild Dunes, near Charleston, S.C. In a second-round match against qualifying medalist Ed Hopkins, Templeton held a 2-up lead through 13 holes. Hopkins battled back to tie the match after the 15th hole, but then Templeton aced the par-3 16th to go 1-up.

Templeton could have won the match with a par at the par-5 18th, but he three-putted from 40 feet.

"I had a sorry putt over a hump," Templeton said. "I can still see it (a four-foot par putt twisting out of the hole). It liked to have driven me crazy for three or four months."

Hopkins won in extra holes and went on to face Oehmig in the finals.

"That would have been so great if we'd played each other," Templeton said. "But it wasn't to be."

Perhaps Templeton could have kept his old friend from making the history books at Wild Dunes. Oehmig defeated Hopkins for his record third U.S.

Senior Amateur title. And at 69, he became the oldest winner in the tournament's history.

Oehmig and Templeton remained playing partners until poor health intervened, but their friendship endured. In 1998, Oehmig gave up golf at 82 after hip replacement surgery. "It just wasn't fun anymore," he said. Oehmig later battled prostate cancer that spread to his right hip.

Templeton, too, was treated for cancer in 2000; he had part of a lung removed and endured chemotherapy. Though he continued to go to Creeks Bend for an hour or two every day, doctors wouldn't allow him to play golf.

Both men faced their illnesses with courage and grace, just as they faced their battles on the golf course. And as usual, both were there for one another, each encouraging the other to meet his respective challenge head on.

"Ira's been through a pretty trying experience," Oehmig said. "He has a great attitude. He's really been an inspiration. I hope he never loses his cockiness. He encourages me and I encourage him."

"We talk almost every day," Templeton said. "We've supported one another."

The admiration that Oehmig and Templeton had for one another and their respective golf games never wavered.

"Lew is a real gentleman," Templeton said. "He's an unusual person, really. There's nothing you can really ly say bad about him. He's just always done what he's supposed to do.

"And his golf swing; it was just perfect. It was just so slow, and with perfect rhythm. He would just intimidate his opponents. Because it was every tee shot down the middle and every shot on the green."

"Ira had a fine swing," Oehmig said. "But his putting was absolutely miraculous. He had a magic touch with that putter. Simply because he had the confidence that he was going to make everything he drew back at."

Years after he won his last trophy, Lew Oehmig paid Ira Templeton the highest tribute. If not for his old adversary, Oehmig's place in amateur golf history might not be so lofty.

"He inspired in you a desire to beat him," Oehmig said. "He was always so full of conversation, so entertaining. And so confident. He always brought out the best in me."

CHAPTER 5

SENIOR SUCCESS

"Two weeks before the 1972 U.S. Senior Amateur, I played with Bill Hyndman, who was a great amateur player, in the [PGA Tour's] Philadelphia Classic. I knew Lew was getting ready to play in his first Senior Amateur, and that Bill would be playing in it. I told Bill I had a good friend from Chattanooga who was going to be playing in his first one, and that he's a real good player. He said, 'What's his name?' I said, 'Lew Oehmig.' He said, 'I never heard of him.' And I said, 'You will.'"

—Larry White

For years, Lew Oehmig was one of the country's best amateurs, but not many golfers outside Tennessee knew it. Business and family commitments kept him from playing the national amateur circuit.

"I had a family to raise and I had a job to do," Oehmig said. "I couldn't always get away and play in those things. They [employers] were very good to me to let me play in as many tournaments as I did. Sometimes, it bothered my conscience taking off as much as I did. I guess I might have stayed with [business] longer than I should have."

Once Oehmig reached senior status, he quickly made up for lost time. The United States Golf Association classifies a senior amateur as any player who reaches his 55th birthday before Oct. 2. A senior professional, as determined by the USGA and PGA Tour, reaches that status if he turns 50 before July 8.

That meant Oehmig couldn't play senior amateur tournaments until he was 55, and he was actually 56 by the time he played in his first USGA Senior, in 1972. Before that, he had plenty of warmup competition in the Tennessee Senior Amateur.

In the early days of the state senior amateur, the TGA considered a senior to be any player at least 50. Oehmig took full advantage, winning five straight tournaments from 1969-1973. Twice in that span, in 1970 and 1971, he also won the state amateur, a rare feat that many think will never be matched. Since that time, and after the senior amateur took a five-year hiatus (some say because of Oehmig's dominance), the TGA has raised the minimum age for senior competition to 55.

All that time spent in the heat of competition and all those trophies he took home steeled Oehmig for national and international seniors competition. From 1972 until he retired from competitive golf in the early '90s, he gave a glimpse of what he might have been as a younger man. Oehmig played in 19 U.S. Senior Amateurs, qualified for match play 18 times, won a record three tournaments (1972, 1976, 1985) and finished runner up (1974, 1977, 1979) a record three times. Oehmig's last victory was the most remarkable, for it came when he was 69 years old, making him the oldest winner in the tournament's history. That record, say some of Oehmig's contemporaries, may never be matched.

"You win those sorts of tournaments in your 50s," said Lew Conner, a Nashville attorney, long-time friend and admirer of Oehmig's and a frequent competitor in senior amateur events. "If you get to play in those events in your 60s, you're excited to death. Winning at nearly 70 years old is implausible to me. I don't think that will ever be done again. You could give Tiger Woods his amateur status back at 69, and I don't think he could win the U.S. Senior Amateur."

Oehmig was also a three-time runner up in the tournament, which no one else has ever been. His six appearances in the finals are also a record.

Oehmig didn't limit his success to the U.S. Senior Amateur. He also won the International Seniors Championship in Gleneagles, Scotland, in 1976 and was runner up the next year. He also qualified for eight U.S. Senior Opens. In 1982, Oehmig won the United States Senior Golf Association championship.

Twice, in 1972 and 1976, Oehmig was chosen by *Golf Digest* as the nation's top-ranked senior golfer.

"When Lew Oehmig's wedge and putter are working—which they are more often than not—the 60-

year-old Tennessean is virtually unbeatable in senior golf," wrote John P. May in the February, 1977, edition of *Golf Digest.* "Twice last summer Oehmig turned loose a steady stream of accurate shots with his reliable short-game clubs to win two important senior championships—the USGA Senior at Cherry Hills in Denver and the International Senior Amateur in Scotland."

Oehmig's game held up longer than that of perhaps any high-level amateur in history. In 1978, at 62, he won his record seventh Chattanooga Men's Metro championship. In 1986, then 70, Oehmig won the Tennessee Senior Open.

"His game didn't fall off as he got older," said Oehmig's old friend Bill Campbell, who won two U.S. Senior Amateurs, including one in 1979, when he turned back Oehmig. "He was a better senior than he was a younger player because he loved the game so much and applied himself. He didn't burn out. He didn't play all the time. He only played when he wanted to."

1972—The First USGA Senior Amateur Title

Just as his friend Larry White had predicted, if no one had heard of Lew Oehmig before the 1972 U.S. Senior Amateur, they certainly had after that tournament was over. In winning his first USGA event at Sharon Golf Club in Sharon Center, Ohio, Oehmig pulled off a series of remarkable rallies, winning three

Lew Oehmig poses with his trophy from the
1972 USGA Senior Amateur Championship in Sharon, Ohio.

of his matches in extra holes.

"If Walter Mitty had fantasied winning a national golf championship, even he would have stopped short of conjuring the miracles that Lew Oehmig wrought during the week in September when he won the USGA Senior," wrote Frank Hannigan in *Golf Journal*.

Oehmig was nearly bumped from his first U.S. Senior Amateur in the second round. Down two holes with five to play against Ed Meister of Willoughby, Ohio, Oehmig seemed doomed when he hit his second shot into the water on the 14th hole. But after Meister missed the green and made bogey, Oehmig halved the hole after knocking a 40-yard wedge within concession range.

Instead of being three down with four holes to play, Oehmig was down just two. He evened the match with a birdie at No. 17 and won with another birdie on the first playoff hole.

Tournament favorite Bill Hyndman, who had told White in a PGA Tour event earlier that summer that he'd never heard of Oehmig, knew all about him after their semifinal round match. Hyndman seemed certain of closing out Oehmig on the 17th hole. He led, 1-up, and had already made birdie. But Oehmig drained a clutch eight-foot putt for a birdie and a halve.

On the 18th, Oehmig hit a beautiful 7-iron to four feet and made the putt for a birdie that sent the match into extra holes. On the 20th hole, Oehmig made a 20-footer for par as Hyndman made bogey and lost the match. Oehmig made five birdies and shot 32 on the incoming nine.

Those matches seemed like blowouts compared to the championship match against Ernie Pieper of San Juan Bautista, Calif. Oehmig was 1-down on the 18th hole, but rolled in a 25-foot birdie putt to send the match to extra holes, where he won on the 20th hole with a two-putt par. Earlier in the match, Oehmig, always a great long-range putter, made birdies from 30 feet and 25 feet.

Oehmig's exploits impressed Hannigan, the former USGA executive director and current rules analyst for ABC. "Oehmig is not only a fantastic putter; he very often knocks the ball up close to the hole," wrote Hannigan in *Golf Journal.* "During the week at Sharon, he played 128 holes [including 36 holes of stroke play qualifying] in 1-under par—truly a glorious record on the longest [6,750] course ever used for a USGA Senior Championship.

"His match against Hyndman must be considered— until something better comes along—the apotheosis of senior amateur golf."

1976—No. 2 Is Just as Sweet

Oehmig needed a bit of help to turn back John Richardson, a long-hitting former hockey player competing in his first U.S. Senior Amateur at Cherry Hills in Denver.

Oehmig had been having back trouble, and Warren

Smith, the head professional at Cherry Hills, recommended a doctor, Harold Magoun.

"The man really helped me," Oehmig told the *Denver Post*. "I understand it is the same doctor who worked on Lee Trevino and got him back on tour."

Magoun had helped Trevino, who found out about the doctor through Smith.

Oehmig built what proved to be an insurmountable lead in the early stages of the round, winning holes 5-9 to go 4-up. Oehmig made a clutch 10-footer to preserve a par and a halve at No. 9.

Richardson had his chances to chip away. Oehmig missed an 18-inch par putt and gave back a hole at No. 10. Richardson reached the par-5 11th hole in two and made a birdie, but Oehmig matched it the old fashioned way, knocking a wedge tight for his third shot.

The match ended after Oehmig hit a 4-iron to 12 feet at the par-3 15th and Thompson buried his shot in a bunker.

"I just got off playing lousy," Richardson told the *Denver Post*. "... Actually, if he misses on nine, and I get him on 11 ... But I didn't win that hole [No. 9]. He just got ahead and kept tagging pars. You do that and you're not going to get beat."

Oehmig's match was typical of his play, as he overcame some shaky short putting to win handily. In 15 holes, he missed just two greens, and those by just a few feet. He had five conceded birdies, all but one of them within 10 feet, lost just two holes and three-putted for his only bogeys.

"I never did feel sure about the match," Oehmig told *Golf World.* "John is explosive. He could have birdied everything, he hits it so far."

Oehmig came away with a great impression of Cherry Hills, where Arnold Palmer rallied for his only U.S. Open victory in 1960.

"This is a super course," he told the press after his victory. "I intend to come back to watch the [U.S.] Open in 1978 and see how the pros play it."

Upon hearing that, USGA Seniors committee chairman Eugene Pulliam couldn't resist adding a comment of his own.

"They won't play much better than you did today," Pulliam said.

Winning the Metro—The Old Man Can Still Play

Oehmig won his first Chattanooga Men's Metro Amateur as an 18-year-old senior at Baylor School in a fateful summer where he introduced himself to Tennessee golf with an upset of the great Emmett Spicer in the Tennessee Amateur. In 1978, at age 62, he won his seventh, a record.

There are few better examples of longevity in golf. Has anyone ever won a tournament and then won it again 44 years later? How many golfers won the same tournament 23 years apart? Oehmig's last victory in the Metro had been in 1955. "I hadn't been able to play in many of these things for various reasons,"

Oehmig told the *Chattanooga News-Free Press* in 1978.

That year, the Metro was played at Battlefield Golf and Country Club. After 36 holes, four players, Oehmig, Mike Jenkins, Malcolm Martin and Harold Lane, were tied for the lead at 144. Jenkins, who would later become president of the Chattanooga District Golf Association and creator/tournament director of the Chattanooga TPC, was in the final group that day and remembers the round well.

"Harold was sick," Jenkins said. "He had a terrible cold and could hardly hold his head up. And we were playing 36 holes [on Sunday] in July."

Oehmig took what seemed to be a commanding, five-shot lead on the front nine of the final round, but Lane, sick as he was, rallied with five birdies to catch him. His 30-foot putt for birdie on No. 18 forced a playoff.

"When I stood on 18, I was actually hoping Harold would make that putt because he had played so well," Oehmig told the *News-Free Press*. "But darn, I sure didn't know that would tie him with me."

Whatever juice Lane found in regulation holes was gone by the playoff, which didn't take long to finish. Lane hit his tee shot on No. 1 into the 18th fairway. A local rule called for any shot from the first tee that landed in the 18th fairway to be dropped into the rough at No. 1. Lane did so, but his ball sunk into the deep grass. He hit his second shot left of the green and couldn't save par.

Oehmig, meanwhile, was sealing the deal with one of his favorite weapons—the fairway wood. No. 1 at Battlefield is a monstrous starting hole at 445 yards. Oehmig split the middle with his drive and needed a 3-wood to get home in two. He two-putted from 20 feet for the victory.

"It's not a disgrace to lose to that man," Lane told the *News-Free Press*.

1985—A Record That Will Never Be Broken?

Oehmig and Ed Hopkins, finalists in the 1985 U.S. Senior Amateur, were well acquainted with one another long before that match, which was played at Isle of Palms, S.C., on the beautiful Wild Dunes course. Oehmig and Hopkins had been friendly foes on the golf course for more than 30 years, dating back to the Champions Cup matches in Houston that were put on by Jimmy Demaret and Jackie Burke.

Like Oehmig, who was eight years his senior, Hopkins had a long and distinguished amateur career. He played in 11 U.S. Amateurs, reaching the quarter-finals in 1955. In 1980, he advanced to the semifinals of the Senior Amateur. A year after reaching that pinnacle, Hopkins underwent heart surgery, and his doctor advised him to give up golf.

That advice went unheeded as Hopkins, with the help of a pacemaker, continued to play high-level golf, winning two Curtis Person Senior Amateur titles.

Hopkins shot 69-74 and was the qualifying medalist at Wild Dunes. The field of 32 that survived to match play included seven former champions. After one round, only Bill Hyndman, Ed Updegraff and Oehmig remained.

Oehmig, much as he did in 1972, when he won his first Senior Amateur, was playing a game of survive and advance in his early matches. He needed 20 holes to beat Charles Sullivan of Swampscott, Mass., in the first round and it took another 20 holes to turn back Chris Kappas of Ponte Vedra Beach, Fla., in the second round.

Oehmig won twice more before facing Clifford Taylor of Spring Lake, Mich., in the semifinals. Taylor had been hard on former Senior Amateur champions in the tournament, already disposing of Hyndman and Dale Morey. Oehmig prevailed, 2 and 1, and advanced to the finals, where he would play Hopkins.

Hopkins was challenged only once on his way to the final, coincidentally enough by Ira Templeton, Oehmig's long-time friend and playing partner from Chattanooga. Templeton aced the par-3 16th hole and rallied to send the match into extra holes. But on the second playoff hole, he three putted, giving Hopkins the victory.

That was the closest Templeton and Oehmig, combatants in so many high-level golf tournaments, came to playing one another in a USGA event.

There was something magical about the 20th hole for

Lew Oehmig, left, receives the first-place trophy at the 1985 U.S. Senior Amateur. On right is Ed Hopkins, who lost to Oehmig in extra holes.

Oehmig. It was there he defeated Hopkins for his third senior title.

"He's been beating me for years and years," Oehmig told *Golf Journal* after the match. "He finally let a little sympathy creep into his heart."

Hopkins, who never won the tournament, wasn't too disheartened by losing to his old friend.

"We're all just happy to be here," he told *Golf Journal*. "It's the competition that keeps us going."

Oehmig would keep going another five years in the U.S. Senior Amateur, playing his last tournament in 1990 at 74. Remarkably, he made another deep run in 1987, winning three matches and playing John Richardson in the semifinals. Richardson, who had lost to Oehmig in the 1976 finals, gained a measure of revenge with a 5 and 4 victory.

Oehmig won his first-round match in 1988 before losing. First-round match-play ousters in 1989 and 1990 helped convince him his time of competing for the championship had come to an end.

Three That Got Away

Amazingly, Oehmig had a chance to win a third of the 18 U.S. Senior Amateurs in which he qualified for match play. If not for Dale Morey and his good friend Bill Campbell, he might have.

Oehmig was the first to tangle with Morey, from High Point, N.C., in a championship match. The year was 1974, and Morey was a rookie on the senior circuit, having just turned 55. But Morey was no stranger to competition. In the '40s, he played on the PGA Tour, but later regained his amateur status. He also played professional basketball in the fledgling days of what would become the National Basketball Association. Morey knew how to compete.

Morey got off to a quick start at the Harbour Town Links in Hilton Head, S.C., winning four of the first five holes. But Oehmig rallied in typical fashion. He cut the margin to 2-down on the par-4 12th. Morey had hit the green in regulation, 18 feet from the hole. Oehmig missed the green and his ball came to rest about 45 feet from the hole. With a deft stroke of his deadly wedge, Oehmig sent the ball toward the cup, where it took one bounce and dove in for a winning birdie.

Oehmig also won No. 13, and heading into No. 14, was just one down. But that's where disaster struck. Oehmig hit his ball in the hazard line, and inadvertently grounded his club. A rules official on the scene declared Morey the winner of the hole. Shaken, Oehmig hit poor tee shots on the next two holes and conceded the match at No. 16.

Oehmig and Morey hooked up again in 1977 at Salem Country Club in Peabody, Mass. Again, Morey got off to a great start, winning three of the first five holes. Oehmig trimmed the margin to 2-up after eight holes, but Morey took the momentum back at No. 9 when he saved par from 30 yards off the green and

Oehmig three-putted.

In 1979 at Chicago Golf Club, Oehmig lost 2 and 1 to Campbell, who will never forget the plane ride home. It so happened that Oehmig and Campbell were on the same flight.

"I was sitting there quietly and the captain came on and announced that the new senior amateur champion was on the plane," Campbell said. "You know how he knew. Lew put him up to it. He didn't mention that the runner up was sitting back there too, a guy who was a ranking player and had done better than I had. But that was Lew. He was always gracious, always generous and always good natured."

One Last Taste of Victory in Tennessee

The headline on the front page of the May 21, 1986, edition of the *Chattanooga Times* trumpeted yet another miraculous Oehmig accomplishment. "Sweet Lew comes through," the headline said, referring to yet another improbable victory for the ageless wonder, this one coming in the Tennessee PGA Senior Open at Signal Mountain Golf and Country Club.

Oehmig never won the Tennessee Open, but he came through in the senior version by virtue of a playoff victory over his long-time friend and playing partner, Ira Templeton.

Oehmig was the tournament's first round leader after shooting 68, but a second-round 73 left him tied at 1-under-par 141. That sent the tournament into extra holes.

Templeton, never one to hold back, smacked a pair of drivers to the par-5 first hole, but his eagle putt stopped six inches short. Oehmig, over the green in 2, pitched to two feet and made a birdie to halve the hole.

The playoff continued to the short, par-4 second hole, and after Templeton missed a 12-footer for birdie, Oehmig rolled in a putt of about eight feet for the win.

The victory was yet another byproduct of a new putting grip Oehmig had adopted the previous fall, when he won his record third U.S. Senior Amateur. Oehmig's unusual grip featured a standard left-hand placement, but something totally unique with his right hand. Oehmig placed the first three fingers on top of the shaft, then braced his little finger against the bottom of the grip.

"It makes the right arm and hand work like a piston," Oehmig told Eddie Davidson of the *Chattanooga Times*. "I started using it last year at Wild Dunes [site of the U.S. Senior] and I'm putting so well with it, the USGA will probably declare it illegal."

The Secret to Longevity

As Oehmig's tinkering with his putting grip showed, he never stopped learning about golf. And he was willing to do whatever it took to remain competitive.

That partially explains why Oehmig won tournaments for so long. But there are other reasons.

The most important reason could be genes. Oehmig

comes from a family of long livers. His father, W.G., lived until he was 90. Two aunts lived to more than 100. Oehmig and his three brothers were still going strong into their 80s.

"It was all very simple," Oehmig said. "Good clean living. Seriously, I suppose longevity was something I was born with. And Mother Nature might have given me that swing—the sense of timing and coordination were sort of built in, I guess. Some people have it more than others. With me, it was God-given ability and it was certainly an asset."

Blessed as he was, Oehmig did all he could to preserve and even improve upon his gifts.

"I used to do a lot of exercises to build myself up," Oehmig said. "I was a skinny, puny little guy. I had to work to build up my physical capability. I'm still doing it today. That has a lot to do with at least my ability to keep going. It's so important. I think everyone should participate in something to keep physically fit."

Oehmig was in tune to the value of weight training 40 years before it became standard in college and professional athletics. *Chattanooga Times* golf writer Al Sharp noticed Oehmig's work with the weights in the summer of 1936.

"If you happened to be at the Chattanooga Golf and Country Club Sunday, you probably admired the build of sun-tanned Lew Oehmig," Sharp wrote. "… You were bound to notice his calves, constructed along the lines of a jumper or toe dancer. ... And after seeing him knock the cover off the ball a couple of times with driver or iron, you started wondering about the shoulders and especially the wrists. A glance showed you that Oehmig's forearms, although not like Popeye's, and his wrists look just as powerful as his iron shots. And they are. But they just didn't grow that way.

"... Oehmig has been working out with dumbbells ever since he was a little fellow. The reason, his father, W.G. Oehmig, Jr., explained, was that Lew suddenly shot up toward the sky when he was four, and weight went into height. Which left Lew without the sturdiness and heftiness of the other Oehmig boys—Von, Bill and Dan."

"I realized I wasn't athletically constructed like my brothers—they were all strong," Oehmig said. "I built myself up to play quarterback [at Baylor School] and it helped me in golf."

Oehmig lifted weights all his life, but also swung a specially designed weighted club, which he thought had all sorts of benefits.

"The weighted club was a factor," Oehmig said. "I pick that old club up every now and then and wonder how I swung the damn thing because it was so heavy. But it was valuable to stretch your golf muscles. It also helped in keeping my rhythm and timing. That's so important in a golf swing."

As Oehmig kept on winning over the years, more and more people began to realize that it wasn't by accident.

119

Oehmig shared some of his theories in the February 1977 edition of *Golf Digest*.

"Seniors tend to restrict their swings as they get older," Oehmig told the magazine. "I think they should strive for as long a backswing as possible while keeping control and a full extension of the arms—especially the left—through and after impact. This keeps your muscles alive, so you can put a forceful swing on the ball."

Few people this side of Sam Snead put so forceful a swing on the ball so far into their senior years.

*Lew and Mary Oehmig at their home. Mary is wearing Lew's medals
from his three USGA Senior Amateur Championships,
which were made into a necklace*

CHAPTER 6

HONORS

"And so tonight, even more than his unique record of golf victories and competitive longevity, we are celebrating, in essence, Lew's heart, his character, his values—all that he stands for. We all know that golf has been on a great roll; but amid the accompanying commercial binge, we should be ever mindful of what makes our sport so different from most others, and better. Lew Oehmig exemplifies that difference."

—Bill Campbell

I f there was one gap in Lew Oehmig's golfing resume, it was the fact that he never won a major national amateur tournament until he was a senior. That kept him from earning consideration to represent his country in the Walker Cup matches, which he would have dearly loved to do.

Oehmig managed to play in six U.S. Amateurs over the years and often competed in the Southern Amateur, but never won either. For the most part, family and business considerations limited him to state and local tournaments.

Thus, it came as a surprise to Oehmig in 1977 when

Lew Oehmig (front) with the 1977 U.S. Walker Cup team.

the USGA contacted him to ask if he would perform a very special task.

"They said they wanted me to be the [non-playing] captain of the Walker Cup team," said Oehmig, who was 61 at the time and had already won a pair of U.S. Senior Amateurs. "I was surprised. I just figured they didn't have anyone else that year to head the team."

Not so, said Oehmig's long-time friend Bill Campbell, a former USGA president and Walker Cup player.

"He was the first non-Walker Cup player or U.S. Amateur champion to captain a team," Campbell said. "I always took that as a great compliment. He was chosen out of a broad range of golfers because of his sterling qualities and his golf record as a senior."

Oehmig did not disappoint.

In 1977, the Great Britain and Ireland side was intent on breaking a long string of futility. No GBI team had ever won on American soil. The matches were to be played in late August at storied Shinnecock Hills Golf Club in Southhampton, N.Y., a course that reminded the GBI players of home.

"… There is a first time for just about everything," wrote GBI captain Sandy Saddler in the USGA's Walker Cup program, "and perhaps this will be our year when, to borrow a term from England's national game, cricket, we shall break our duck."

Oehmig wasn't about to let any ducks be broken on his watch, especially with such a star-studded team at his disposal: There was Bill Sander, the reigning U.S. Amateur champion who had made the cut in the 1977 Masters; John Fought of BYU, who would win the Amateur days after the Walker Cup and who had made the cut in the U.S. Open and Masters that year; Scott Simpson, who played for Southern Cal and had won the 1976 and 1977 NCAA championships; Gary Hallberg, the 1977 North and South Amateur champion who played for Wake Forest; Lindy Miller of Oklahoma State, who was low amateur in the 1977 U.S. Open; long-time amateur stalwart Jay Sigel; 1975 U.S. Amateur champion Fred Ridley–plus Richard Siderowf, Vance Heafner and Michael Brannan.

Though Oehmig had a talented team, he prepared for

the matches as intently as he had for any tournament in his life, studying each player's record, analyzing their particular strengths and weaknesses and poring over every hole at Shinnecock. He even put in some calls to old friends, including former Walker Cup captains Campbell and Charlie Coe. A conversation with Jackie Burke was particularly helpful. Burke had served as Ryder Cup captain in 1973 as the U.S. had prevailed, 18-13, in Muirfield, Scotland. He also played on four Ryder Cup teams in the '50s and was obviously well-versed in international team play strategy.

"He gave me some ideas that I do not believe have been used in Walker Cup play before," Oehmig told the *Houston Chronicle*.

Undaunted by the task ahead, the GBI side, dubbed "Sandy's Tartan Army" by the *Scottish Daily Press*, played subtle mind games before the matches began.

"They don't look like much," said Peter McEvoy, then the reigning British Amateur champion. "I can't remember when I've been less impressed."

Said Saddler of his team, "If they produce the golf on Friday and Saturday that they have all week, we'll be home and dry by Saturday night."

That wasn't to be. The U.S. team won 9 of a possible 12 points the first day, taking three of four matches in foursomes and six of eight singles matches. McEvoy's words came back to haunt him as he bore the brunt of the beating. He and future Masters champion Sandy Lyle lost 4 and 3 in foursomes to Heafner and Fought. And McEvoy shot a fat 78 in losing his singles match to Miller.

On Saturday, the GBI team rallied for a 2-2 split in foursomes, but the U.S. needed just a win and a tie in singles play to win its third straight Walker Cup. Miller won an early match, leaving the heroics to 19-year-old Gary Hallberg, who whipped the bedraggled McEvoy 4 and 3. All McEvoy's pre-match prognostication had earned him was an 0-4 record as the U.S. won 16-8 in one of the most lopsided victories in Walker Cup history.

Oehmig had a decision to make before the final day's singles rounds. He had planned even before leaving for Shinnecock Hills that he would evenly distribute playing time, and true to that strategy, kept Simpson and Heafner out of singles competition. The decision was questioned by some, but Oehmig never backed down.

"No, we weren't trying to be polite by not playing Simpson and Haefner," Oehmig said in an Associated Press account of the match. "Like Dick Siderowf told the team last night: 'Let's not take any prisoners.' We wanted to win everything we could, and we nearly did. But I felt that if any of the players were good enough to be on the Walker Cup team, they were all good enough to play three matches, and that's why I left Vance and Scott out of the last match.

"This just shows how well-trained and well-prepared the young golfers in the United States are. They may be young, but they've got more match experience than many of the older British players."

Simpson had no problem with sitting out the final round, as he shared with Oehmig by letter a few days after the match.

"I'm sorry you got a bit of criticism for not playing Vance and I (sic) the last match, Lew," wrote Simpson, who would go on to win the 1987 U.S. Open. "I understood completely. I wish I could have played four like everyone else, but having everyone play at least three matches was more important to me. ... I'm also happy that we won, because it really was a good team with a super captain."

Other players also praised the work of Oehmig.

"For me, the Walker Cup was an experience I shall never forget," wrote John Fought in a letter to the man he referred to only as "captain." "As a boy, I used to dream of being chosen for such an honor. Representing the U.S. and winning gave me a great deal of satisfaction. You played a major role in the team's success and I thank you for doing the wonderful job you did."

Herbert Warren Wind, the legendary golf writer who covered the match for the USGA's *Golf Journal*, also praised Oehmig's efforts.

"The American captain, Lew Oehmig, who is our present Senior Amateur Champion, kept a very low profile but ran his team beautifully," wrote Wind in *Golf Journal*. "It was typical of his astute judgement that Fought and Miller, the two men he chose to play four times — both mornings and afternoons — each won four points. While this may have been the least exciting Walker Cup Match since 1961, first-class leadership was essential, for, as was mentioned earlier, this was a good-looking British team filled with players with nice, sound swings who hit the ball with the tempo that marks a superior shotmaker."

The USGA was pleased with the job Oehmig did.

"Officially, I want to congratulate you on being the winning captain of the 1977 Walker Cup matches," wrote USGA president Harry W. Easterly in a letter to Oehmig. "You did an outstanding job of getting the most out of the players. More than any year I can remember, you served as a link between the players and the officials, which served to make the whole affair even more pleasant than it might have been.

"… I meant what I said at the prize presentation: that Lew Oehmig should be the permanent captain of the Walker Cup team."

Oehmig thoroughly enjoyed his week at Shinnecock Hills, as he shared with the USGA in an exhaustive post-match report.

"In closing, let me say that it came as a great surprise to receive the call from Harry Easterly and Sandy Tatum inviting me to be the non-playing captain of the U.S. Walker Cup Team," Oehmig wrote. "It was a tremendous honor which I accepted with some reservations and a great deal of humility after conferring with my two good friends and former Walker Cup Captains, Bill Campbell and Charlie Coe, both of whom gave me the benefit of their sound counsel and advice.

"The members of the American Team were a fine group of gentlemen with tremendous enthusiasm, great golfing ability and a 'gung-ho' attitude whose motto was 'to take no prisoners'—all of which contributed to our fine victory, a particularly sweet one since the magnificent Shinnecock Hills Golf Course with its rolling green fairways, well-placed bunkers, and undulating greens seemed to have so much of the flavor of Scotland and the courses of England that the British were openly confident of winning."

The Honors Circle

When a group of Chattanooga businessmen conceived a plan to build a world-class golf course in the late '70s, they quickly realized that in order to see their dream to fruition, they would need help. There was only one logical person from whom to seek that assistance—John T. "Jack" Lupton, a successful businessman and avid golfer who, as a member of Augusta National, knew a thing or two about world-class golf courses.

As it turned out, Lupton shared their dream, and even took it a step farther. Before construction could begin on land that the partners deemed worthy in

Above: The 18th hole at the Honors Course is named for Lew Oehmig.
Below: Lew Oehmig's plaque at the Honors Circle, located
in front of the Honors Course clubhouse.

nearby Ooltewah, a name for the course had to be determined. Lupton had more than just a name in mind. He had a concept.

"Part of the early planning involved settling on a name for the new course," wrote G.Z. "Bome" Patten in *The Birth of Greatness: The Story of the Creation of The Honors Course*. "Suffice it to say that there were many suggestions. Jack solved the problem quickly and decisively. 'It will be known as The Honors Course,' Lupton said. 'We are honoring amateur golf at the local, state and national levels—so let's go with The Honors Course.' ... All agreed that this was an outstanding name and concept."

Lupton's inspiration for The Honors Course was Bobby Jones, under whose charismatic spell Lupton fell after being invited to join Augusta National in the '60s. Jones, long since removed from his glory days as America's greatest career amateur, was in the clutches of a debilitating illness by the time Lupton got to know him well, but though his body could no longer do what it used to, his mind was sharp and clear. Lupton was captivated by Jones' warm personality, his storytelling and all for which he stood as a lifelong amateur.

Thus when The Honors was opened in 1983, it was done so primarily as a tribute to Jones, but also to other great amateurs who came after him.

Visitors to The Honors quickly realize they have come to a shrine of amateur golf. Outside the club-house is the Honors Circle, which in the beginning paid tribute to just five people, all great players, all Tennesseans. Lew Oehmig was among those five, and he was in esteemed company: Polly Boyd, father of founding Honors Course member Lew Boyd and perhaps Chattanooga's first great golfer who won four Tennessee Amateurs. Judy Eller Street, who came from Tennessee's first family of golf, the Ellers, and who distinguished herself with seven Tennessee Amateur championships, two women's Southern Amateur titles, a national collegiate title, two USGA girls junior victories and two appearances on the Curtis Cup team. Betty Rowland Probasco, a transplanted Kentuckian who won four amateur championships in her home state, seven more in Tennessee, a Southern Amateur, a national collegiate title, and was captain of the 1982 Curtis Cup team. Cary Middlecoff, who won four straight Tennessee Amateurs from 1940-43 and later won two U.S. Opens and a Masters.

"The Honors Circle was conceived to honor the people who have established themselves as the greatest amateurs in this state," Lupton said.

Lupton and Oehmig had a long-time association, dating back to the early '50s when Lupton, who had taken up the game only in his 20s, "couldn't play a lick," by his own admission, and yet was befriended by Oehmig.

"I'd had an association with Lew's brother Dan," Lupton said. "And that's how I became friends with Lew. It was all through golf. He quickly became a real hero to me. He would just as soon play with me as he would Arnold Palmer. It didn't make a bit of difference to him. He just enjoyed the game of golf."

Lupton became captivated by Oehmig's grace and skill, as did everyone who watched Oehmig play.

"I've always called him the maestro," Lupton said. "Because to me, he was just exactly like a maestro leading an orchestra, with that fabulous swing of his that had such rhythm and tempo."

There was never any question that once The Honors was built Oehmig would be among its initial group of honorees. In addition to plaques detailing their accomplishments at the Honors Circle, the five original members also had holes on The Honors Course dedicated to their memory.

"It was ladies first," Lupton said. "I gave Mrs. Probasco the choice, and she picked what has become our signature hole, No. 9. Then it was Lew's turn, so I called him, and he said, 'I pick 18.' There were 17 holes to pick from at that point. I asked him why he picked 18. He said, 'Because it's the last hole you play and the last you remember.' And he was right. No. 18 is a helluva hole."

Years later, Oehmig laughed at the recollection of picking No. 18, a 451-yard par-4 that was chosen in 2000 by *Golf Magazine* as one of the top 500 holes in the world. "It was one of the most troubling holes on the golf course," he said. "I figured if I had my name on that hole, people would remember me. I just hope they don't go away cussing me."

The concept of the Honors Circle was a surprise to Oehmig, despite the fact that his brother Dan was a founding member and he was a charter member.

"I didn't know anything about the Honors Circle until Jack pulled it off," Oehmig said. "There were a lot of very deserving people honored there. It's quite an honor to be out there and seen by so many people."

Tennessee Golf's Highest Honor

In the early '90s, a dream of Dick Horton, the executive director of the Tennessee PGA and the Tennessee Golf Association, was realized with the advent of the Tennessee Golf Foundation. Though the foundation was created primarily for the benefit of the game's future in Tennessee—particularly through junior golf programs—it also preserves golf's proud history in the state. One of the Foundation's first official acts was to create the Tennessee Golf Hall of Fame.

Lew Oehmig was a charter inductee into the Hall of Fame, along with three of the players who had been honored years earlier at The Honors Course Honor Circle. Besides Oehmig, Betty Probasco and Cary Middlecoff, four others were among the initial class of inductees: Curtis Person of Memphis, one of the state's all-time best amateurs; Mason Rudolph of Clarksville, who had a solid PGA Tour career; Lou Graham of Nashville, the 1975 U.S. Open winner; and longtime *Nashville Banner* golf writer Dudley "Waxo" Green.

*Lew Oehmig with Betty Probasco at the Tennessee
Golf Hall of Fame induction dinner.*

In January, 1991, Oehmig and Probasco were formally inducted into the hall at a dinner at the Chattanooga Choo Choo. It seemed as though anyone who had ever picked up a club in Chattanooga was in attendance. Bill Campbell, past USGA president and a long-time friend of Oehmig's, was there to introduce Oehmig, and he spoke with sincere admiration.

"Lew was and is a marvel," Campbell said in his presentation speech. Whether he wins or loses the friendly smile and the kind words are always there. Lew Oehmig is forever."

For his part, Oehmig, modest as always, seemed overwhelmed by all the attention, as though his record number of state amateur, state senior amateur and USGA senior championships were hardly worthy of consideration. As far as the public knew, those accomplishments were what earned Oehmig his well-deserved entry into the hall of fame. But there was more. In his own quiet way, very much behind the scenes, Oehmig did as much to ensure the solid growth of Tennessee golf as anyone.

Three times, in 1948, 1957 and 1967, Oehmig served as president of the Tennessee Golf Association, and for more than 40 years, he served the TGA as a board member. On at least two occasions, he helped shape the future of the game in his home state by standing up for what he believed was right.

"Lew Oehmig is the epitome of what the Tennessee Golf Hall of Fame stands for," said Nashville attorney

Lew Conner, a native Chattanoogan who grew up worshiping Oehmig and later became the first chairman of the Tennessee Golf Foundation. "In every way you can be of service to golf, Lew Oehmig was there. No. 1, he was the greatest amateur the state of Tennessee has seen or ever will see. No. 2, he was the president of the TGA on more than one occasion. And of course, he was so instrumental in the structure of Tennessee golf as we know it."

In the late '60s, a long-standing feeling of ill will among Tennessee club professionals and amateurs had risen toward a confrontation of volcanic proportions over the issue of handicapping.

"At that time, we could see the handicapping system coming into play as a source of revenue, and both sides, the pros and amateurs, wanted a part of it," Conner said.

At one meeting between the two sides Conner, who was representing both parties as legal counsel, suggested an equal revenue split. The atmosphere in the room was hostile, until Oehmig stepped up in defense of Conner.

"I would have lost that night except for one person," Conner said. "When Lew stood up and said I was right, the entire mood of the meeting changed, as even the aggressors rethought the subject."

Several months later, another issue was at stake—whether Horton, who had been hired by the club professionals as their executive director, should also take

Mary and Lew Oehmig with Dick Horton.

over leadership of the TGA. Some long-time TGA officers involved in the discussion wondered whether the organization, which had been run by volunteers, could take on the expense of Horton.

"I stood up and backed Dick Horton," Conner said. "I was going to lose because some people were afraid we were going to go broke if we took on Dick's salary. So I told them I'd guarantee the money, that I'd make up any shortfall.

"People kind of laughed at me. How could a young lawyer reach into his pockets and make up any difference? And then Lew stood and said, 'I'll back him.' There were two things people knew about Lew. One, he was as good as his word. Two, he had the money to stand behind his word."

Horton has never forgotten that fateful day.

"While some directors were a bit uneasy that Lew [Conner] also served as legal counsel for the TPGA and maybe some alternative deal was underlining the whole idea, when Lew Oehmig spoke up and told the group he too was in on the guarantee, the motion immediately carried," Horton said. "My introduction to Lew was that when he spoke, everyone listened and respected his judgment. The two Lews who went out on a limb for me fortunately never had to ante up a penny, but my appreciation for Lew Oehmig was quickly cemented since he hardly knew me."

Clearly, Oehmig was as respected in a meeting room as he was on the golf course.

"I was on the TGA board with Lew and also the Southern Golf Association board," said Orvis Milner of Knoxville. "He never just spouted something out and people knew that. When he gave his opinion on something, it was after he had thought it out and looked at the pros and cons of it. And it made a big impact on whatever side he took when he did speak out. He might not say anything for a while. He never just started talking, like some of our people do, including me. As a consequence, he got everybody's attention."

It's impossible to say whether Horton would ever have been allowed to take over the TGA had Conner and Oehmig not intervened. But their insistence that Horton be hired was critical to the organization's future. Under Horton's leadership, the TGA has become a model by which other state associations seek to pattern themselves. Its facilities—including Golf House Tennessee, which houses all the state's governing bodies as well as the Hall of Fame, the Little Course at Aspen Grove and world-class junior golf teaching facilities—all came as a result of Horton's leadership and vision.

Would Tennessee golf be in a nationwide leadership role today had Horton not been hired to guide the TGA?

"Dick was somebody we really needed at the time," Oehmig said. "He was a young guy, he had enthusiasm, he had good ideas. We just saw what he could do for the association, and Lew and I really felt strongly about it.

"The guy who had been handling the job, old Roy Moore, was a good guy and did a wonderful job, but he was getting old. The opportunity to get Dick was too good to pass up, so Lew and I stood up for him. It's pleasing to know after all these years that we were right. Dick Horton is a jewel."

Besides the Tennessee Golf Hall of Fame, Oehmig is also enshrined in several other places of honor, among them the Tennessee Sports Hall of Fame, the Southern

Golf Association Hall of Fame, the Chattanooga Old Timers Sports Hall of Fame and the Lookout Mountain Hall of Fame.

Oehmig's entry into the Tennessee Sports Hall of Fame came in 1973, after he had won eight state amateurs, five state senior amateurs and a U.S. Senior Amateur. He was introduced that night by old friend and opponent Curtis Person, Sr., in a special ceremony that included Jesse Owens as the guest speaker.

In 1981, Oehmig joined some elite company when he became just the eighth inductee into the Southern Golf Association's Hall of Fame. Bobby Jones was the first player enshrined there, and he was followed by, among others, Person and another great career amateur, Billy Joe Patton.

The USGA's Highest Honor

In its media guide, the United States Golf Association describes its Bob Jones Award thusly:

"The Bob Jones Award, presented in recognition of distinguished sportsmanship in golf, is the highest honor bestowed by the United States Golf Association. It has been presented annually since 1955 in commemoration of the vast contribution by Jones to the cause of fair play during and after his playing career, which ended with his retirement from competitive golf at the age of 28 in 1930.

"In establishing the award, the USGA wished to honor not Jones' accomplishments as a player, but

Lew Oehmig holding the Bob Jones Award.

rather his spirit, his qualities as a human being and his attitude toward the game and its players."

Many of the greatest players in history, including Francis Ouimet, Babe Zaharias, Gary Player, Arnold Palmer, Byron Nelson, Jack Nicklaus, Ben Hogan, Gene Sarazen and Tom Watson won the Bob Jones Award.

In 1994, it was only fitting that Lew Oehmig joined that distinguished group. When the call from the USGA came, Oehmig, typically, was truly amazed he had won the award.

"I was completely stunned and overwhelmed when I was notified of the award," Oehmig said. "I thought somebody had made a mistake."

But no mistake had been made. Those who know Oehmig best thought the award was a long time coming.

"My first thought was that it's about time," said Jack Lupton, the Honors Course chairman and a strong USGA supporter. "To me, the Bob Jones Award is what Lew Oehmig is all about. Look at the names on that. It doesn't get any better. It's the pinnacle of achievement in golf."

No one who played with Oehmig doubted he had the qualities that made him more than deserving for the honor.

"He was so courteous on the golf course that his opponents sometimes thought it was fake," said Ira Templeton, Oehmig's long-time friend and playing partner. "He was always a real gentleman. I never saw him display his temper. He's an unusual person, really. There's nothing you can really say bad about him."

"He had a gentlemanly way about him that you rarely associate with an athlete," said Jeff Boehm, unofficial historian for Chattanooga Golf and Country Club. "Certainly not today. He would never do anything to jangle an opponent's concentration."

"The Bob Jones Award is given for distinguished sportsmanship," said Bill Campbell, a past USGA president, long-time friend of Oehmig's, member of the Bob Jones Award committee and, in 1956, also a winner of the honor. "That can be a specific act of sportsmanship or a general pattern. In Lew's case, there have been a lot of specific acts of sportsmanship, but he's a perfect example of the second category. He's a great influence on the rest of us. He's the embodiment of the ideal of the Bob Jones Award."

Oehmig was given the award at a special ceremony during the 100th annual USGA meeting at Scottsdale, Ariz., in January, 1994. After Campbell's opening speech introducing his old friend and Oehmig's heartfelt acceptance remarks, there was hardly a dry eye in the house.

"It was tremendously moving," said King Oehmig, who gave the invocation on his father's big night. "To have your dad receive the highest award in golf, particularly since Bobby Jones was his hero and example ... it was just fantastic."

"One of the highlights of my career was seeing Lew receive the Bob Jones Award from the USGA," said Dick Horton of the TGA. "I made the trip to Arizona for the presentation and it was one of the most meaningful awards I have ever seen a Tennessean receive. The respect that surrounded him was incredible—from all corners of the country."

For Oehmig, the Bob Jones Award was a treasured exclamation mark to what had been an amazing career in the game he loved so dearly all his life.

"I consider this award by far the highest honor I have received in golf," Oehmig said. "It is named for the man I consider to be the greatest player who ever played the game, and a man who was universally known for his fair play. ... The past recipients have been great heroes to me. I feel very humble."

Mary and Lew Oehmig with their grandchildren.

Lew Oehmig (center) with his sons West (left) and King.

147

CHAPTER 7

DISSECTING
A GREAT GAME

"Lew Oehmig understood the game of golf. That's what Cary Middlecoff said about people who could really play. Lew understood the game. He knew he was going to miss some shots. But he hit a lot of great shots. He knew how to play."

—Mason Rudolph

T he man dubbed by the media as "Sweet-Swinging Lew" was never one to brag about his many victories or get overly analytical when it came to discussing his swing or the other facets of his game. In recounting his vast accomplishments, Lew Oehmig uses the word "luck" over and over again, as though his numerous trophies came as a result of so many fortuitous occurrences. But anyone who ever saw Oehmig play, or swing a golf club, knows there was more to Oehmig's game than good fortune. And though Oehmig might be reluctant to speak his own praises, there are plenty of others willing to do it for him.

Here, with the help of some of his friends in golf, is a look at every facet of Oehmig's game.

Probably wound up near the cup.

THE SWING
Ira Templeton

"Lew's swing was just perfect. He had such great rhythm. He never would go through those periods most people go through where they just can't hit it. I'd go through periods where there was nothing I could do to drive it straight. He was always the same. 'Sweet-Swingin' Lew.' That's what some of the guys called him."

Orvis Milner

"It just wasn't fair for a man to strike the ball as well as Lew did."

Mason Rudolph

"I'll never forget the first time I saw him swing that club. I said to myself, 'This guy has a beautiful golf swing.' It was just so simple. I didn't see much that could go wrong with it.

"Lew's swing reminded me of Gene Littler's swing. Both of them were very simple swings. There were no wasted moving parts. It was like Ben Hogan said about the swing: Everything goes to the right going back and to the left going through."

Betty Probasco

"I'm a great admirer of Lew Oehmig and have always been a great admirer of that golf swing. It's just absolutely incredible it's so good. It looks like nothing could ever go wrong with it."

Eli Tullis

"He had the perfect mirror image swing—back and through it was absolutely identical."

Bill Battle

"Lew's swing was picturesque. It was so simple. Every time he stood up there, it was the same."

Erie Ball

"I group Lew Oehmig in with Bobby Jones and Sam Snead as far as their swings were concerned. They all had graceful, natural swings."

Bill Campbell

"His tempo was so good. Lew had a gadget he used to keep in his suitcase—a very short metal driver. It was quite heavy. He'd do this at odd times to extend his arc and exercise his muscles. He always had a good turn, never rushed anything, never took the club back fast. He also had a nice transition at the top—you never saw power being applied.

"Lew's game was built on a reliable, repetitive swing. He had an upright swing and didn't take it back past parallel. It always looked the same. It was what I would call a pure swing like some of the old-timers had. He was a swinger of the golf club as opposed to those who are hitters of the golf ball. He was a natural."

Bill Oehmig

"Lew never tried to kill the ball. He could have gotten more distance, but accuracy was the thing."

Lew Oehmig

"I'd like to take credit for it. But I think the good Lord put the tempo in me and also the desire to do better, to play better and to win."

THE DRIVER
Lew Conner

"Lew was a great driver of the ball for a couple of reasons. One, he cut it, which means he could always find it. And two, he had another gear. When he needed to be long, when he needed a few extra yards, he had that ability."

Buck Johnson

"Lew didn't know the rough existed. I've never seen him in much trouble. He was just a machine. That's all he was. A machine."

Lew Oehmig

"I got in the habit early of cutting the ball and never fully got out of it. I always had a tendency to fade it. I had a hard time hooking the ball; the left side of the golf course was taken out of play automatically. I think it was a flaw in my swing that let the right shoulder come over, that would make the ball fade. When I was playing well and thinking well, I would aim left and let the ball drift back into the middle.

"Keeping the ball in the middle of the fairway is the most important thing in golf."

153

FAIRWAY WOODS
Bobby Greenwood

"He was the best wood player I've ever seen, and I played on the PGA Tour for seven years with some of the best players in the game."

Larry White

"Lew could hit a 4-wood as straight as he could his 8-iron."

Lew Oehmig

Even though I liked to carry a 1 or 2 iron, I always carried three woods, too. But I kept it legal. I always made sure I had 14 clubs in the bag. I liked to have a fairway wood or two in the bag, though I can't remember what I left out. I'm sure it was based on what course I was playing.

"With the fairway woods, I just thought of them like any other club. People always have a tendency to go for more distance and put a little more into the swing. I always just let the club do the work. I never tried to rush it with a fairway wood. It's awfully easy to do if you're not careful."

LONG IRONS

It would be safe to say that the legend of Lew Oehmig began with a long iron. As explained in more detail earlier in this book, Oehmig first came into prominence as a formidable player when he defeated

Emmett Spicer of Memphis in the 1934 Tennessee Amateur. The match, played at Chattanooga Golf and Country Club, came down to the par-3 18th hole. Oehmig used a 1-iron and hit his approach to about a foot.

Spicer credited Oehmig's "guts" after that shot, but his intestinal fortitude had its origins on the practice tee. Oehmig hit countless shots with 1- and 2-irons.

Lew Oehmig

"Fortunately, I had a knack for hitting the long irons. I always carried a 1- or 2-iron. Some people are afraid to hit them because they don't have too much loft on them. But I just recognized the need as a young player to be skilled with the long irons. So I practiced and practiced, and hit ball after ball. I got to where I became pretty proficient with those things. It wasn't an overnight thing.

"If I was going to tell anyone how to hit long irons, I'd tell them to concentrate on the timing and the rhythm. If you try to force the swing, it's hard to hit them. You definitely have to get a feel of the clubhead out there swinging rather than taking your arms and hitting the ball."

SHORT IRONS
Eddie Davidson

"The most remarkable thing about Lew's swing was his tempo; it was the same whether he had a driver in his hand or a 7-iron. Consequently, he always had a good knowledge of how far he was going to hit each club. With the short irons, which are the scoring clubs, that was quite an advantage."

Lew Oehmig

"I spent a lot of time at the golf course [Chattanooga Golf and Country Club] as a youngster. I'd take practice balls and go out on the course. No one would be there in the mornings. I'd practice, say on No. 16. Those big towers were in the distance and it would be a real challenge aiming at them. That's how I got good with my short irons. I hit so many balls as a young kid."

WEDGE PLAY

For years, Oehmig carried an old Wilson R-90 sand wedge. Oehmig and the wedge parted company one year (he can't remember the exact year) when an airline lost his golf bag. He never did get his clubs back. All of them were easily replaced, except the wedge.

Lew Oehmig

"I searched for years to get another wedge like that old R-90. Then First Flight developed a wedge which was very similar and equally as effective. It was a modified Sand Hog. It had a rounded bottom. I worked on it and flattened out that bottom to where it had a bounce similar to the old Wilson."

Eddie Davidson

"When Lew Oehmig had a wedge in his hand, he could hit it close to the hole from anywhere. He was maybe the very best I ever saw with a wedge. He could make people weak with it."

Larry White

"Lew and I were partners in the TGA Two-Man Scramble one year [1975]. We made a ton of birdies and won fairly easily. The highlight of the two days came on a par 5 after I had hit my second shot. He laid up 50 yards short of the green. I went for the green and missed it to the right. We were behind a bunker in four- or five-inch rough. The pin was right against the bunker. You really had to hit a high soft shot to get it close. We went down and looked at my ball. I said 'Lew, I think we might ought to play yours. I don't know if I can hit this shot or not.' He said, 'I can hit it.' I said OK, so he hits it up there about two feet. He was tremendous around the green. That's what impressed me the most, his ability around the green in all sorts of situations. He could really hit that high soft shot."

Buck Johnson

"Lew had the best short game I ever saw. He could make that wedge talk."

Lew Conner

"Lew was the best wedge player I ever played with, and I've spent my life playing with some pretty good ones. He hit it every way he wanted to hit it."

Lew Oehmig

"I practiced an awful lot with the wedge. Old Darden Hampton (a Tennessee Amateur winner and member at Chattanooga Golf and Country Club) was one of the best I'd ever seen with a wedge. I used him as my model. He knew how important it was to handle that wedge.

"It certainly came in handy for me. It made every par-5 a potential birdie opportunity, because I didn't get home to many of the par-5s in two."

PUTTING
Orvis Milner

"Some people said Lew didn't putt it very well. But he hit it so well so often and was so good with a wedge that people just assumed he wasn't a good putter—you can't make everything!"

Jack Lupton

"Lew was one of the greatest lag putters I ever saw. He routinely could knock them in the hole from 40 feet, and he'd almost always get the ball close."

Lew Connor

"Lew always complained about his putting. But he was not a bad putter. When he was winning, he was putting pretty well, because the people he was playing against were very, very good players."

Larry White

"He wasn't a great putter. If he was, he'd have won everything! He still made a ton of good putts, though. A ton of good putts."

Eli Tullis

"He was unbelievable on putts of over 10 feet and circumspect from three feet in. If he had a 20-footer, he most probably would sink it. Give him a four-footer and there was a 50-50 chance he'd miss it. Four feet in was the only weakness in his game."

Eddie Davidson

"I'll never forget one time covering Lew in the Southern Amateur at Druid Hills in Atlanta. On the first hole, Lew hit it to about one or two feet. He stepped up there before his opponent had a chance to give it to him and missed it. The rest of the round, his opponent made him putt out everything, no matter how short they were. Lew was hitting his irons extremely well that day. Every putt he had seemed like it was inside 10 feet and maybe three or four were inside of three feet. He missed a bunch of short putts, but still won 6 and 4. Tee to green, it was one of the best rounds I ever saw, and it shows you how he won so much despite having trouble with the short putts."

Lew Oehmig

"Putting is the secret to the game. If you putt well, you can make up for a lot of miscues with the other shots. So many of my competitors were good putters. Ira Templeton could knock it in from anywhere, and he had confidence he was going to knock them in. I guess I missed so many of them I lost confidence. I was a streak putter. Sometimes I would have lucky streaks and just knock in everything. More often than not, I had problems.

"Through the years, putting technique changed an awful lot. I started out using a lot of wrist in the stroke. Then it became an arm and shoulder swing. It was sort of a metamorphosis. The wristy stroke isn't good under pressure. A lot of good golfers putted that way years ago.

"I was more consistent on long putts than on short putts. It's not as intense as trying to make a four or five footer. 'Feel' best describes how I putted the long ones. On a long putt, I would walk halfway to the hole and take practice swings while looking at the hole. I just thought that was the best way I could get an approximate speed and figure how hard I had to hit it.

"The short putts were different. It became sort of a

problem with me, making those short putts. Then I went to the long putter and all those problems were over. I'd recommend the long putter to anyone. Although most of the guys on the tour, even some of the better amateurs, have tried it and gone back to the standard putter. You don't see many of those long putters on the tour.

"[Throughout my career] I used a lot of different putters. I putted with an old No. 3 First Flight, which is more of a blade putter, for years. Then I used a Ping Anser. I had a basement full of putters at one time.

"The older I got the more my nerves weren't as good as they should have been. But I always remember that I putted best when I was carefree about whether it went in. When you're too concerned about making it, you put more pressure on yourself. You don't stroke it as smoothly."

SAND PLAY
Jack Lupton
"You could put Lew in the sand and you never wondered was he going to get the ball close. You wondered whether he was going to make it or not."

Lew Conner
"Lew was a great sand player. He was a magician with that dadgum club."

Lew Oehmig

"I'll never forget the old pro up at Farmington Country Club, Erie Ball. He helped me more with my sand game than anyone else while I was a student at the University of Virginia. One of the things he told me was not to swing too hard and to make sure I accelerated through the shot."

TROUBLE SHOTS
Jimmy Wittenberg

"He had an amazing ability to recover if he ever did hit a bad shot. You just didn't think there was a chance sometimes, but he had that ability to get out from under trouble."

Larry White

"When he got around the greens, Lew was going to get the ball up and down. You couldn't keep him out of the tournament. He was gonna be there. Coming down the stretch, when good players start missing greens and it was hard to get it up and down, he could get it up and down."

Lew Oehmig

"Again, my wedge saved me a lot. If you missed a green or hit a trap or something, you didn't automatically take a bogey. Other than driving the ball in the fairway, I think the ability to handle the shots 100 yards and in is the most important thing to work on if you want to be good at golf."

MATCH PLAY STRATEGY
Ira Templeton

"Lew Oehmig was a super shotmaker. You can't believe how good he was tee to green. That's why he won so much in match play. It would intimidate the opposition—every shot down the middle and every shot on the green."

Albert Stone, Jr.

"Lew knew his way around. I remember one match we were playing. On a short golf course, you like to shoot at the green first [in match play]. I was trying to lay in behind him on the drives, and he was trying to lay in behind me. It got to the point I don't think we were knocking it more than a couple of hundred yards. Lew never did anything unethical. He was just always a good competitor."

COMPETITIVE DRIVE
Eli Tullis

"Lew was an intense competitor. But you didn't realize it when you were playing him. He'd be walking down the fairway talking to you and you think everything's fine. But when he got over that ball, all that nice conversation left him. He had that wonderful concentration over the ball that few people have."

Billy Ragland

"He was always gracious, win or lose. But he didn't like losing. Not one bit."

Jimmy Wittenberg, Sr.

"Lew was a real good competitor, an intense competitor. But in a friendly way. That's the best way to put it."

Mary Oehmig

"Everyone always remarked at how calmly and graciously Lew took losing. Well, it bothered him more than he let on. I can remember several times driving home—this was before the interstate system was in place—after Lew had lost in a tournament. We'd be driving along, and all of a sudden Lew would step on the brake and just let out a string of language about some putt he'd missed. Then we'd drive on. He'd be OK for a little while, then he'd stop and start hollering again."

SUMMATION

Lew Oehmig has been asked the question countless times. With such a great game, why did he choose to remain an amateur? Why didn't he test himself against the game's best in some of the most prestigious tournaments in the world?

Oehmig had his reasons. Family considerations were foremost among them.

"There just wasn't any money in professional golf at that time," Oehmig said. "I was fortunate enough to do well in business early on in life. Pro golf wouldn't have paid me that kind of money. I also had a family to consider. I felt guilty enough at times leaving them to play the [amateur] golf I did."

Could Oehmig have played—and excelled—on the PGA Tour? Some good golfers who competed against Lew and later went on to play on the tour think so.

"Lew in my opinion was among the top five golfers this state has ever produced," said Mason Rudolph, who is among those five players and had a solid PGA Tour career. "And most of those players played on the tour. There's no way to tell, of course, but Lew's game stacked up with others who played the tour. He just came along at a time when he didn't need to play golf for a living. It was a different deal in those days. The money didn't start getting right until after Jack Nicklaus had come along."

"I remember Hogan telling me that when he was playing, you had to finish in the top 10 just to make $50," said Doug Sanders, who played a money match or two against Oehmig in his day. "Lew Oehmig could make a helluva lot more than that in the business world. But if you're asking could he have played on the tour, my answer is, yeah, he could have done that easily."

Larry White, one of the best players Chattanooga has ever produced, had a great college golf career at the

University of Houston and played the tour for a couple of years. He echoed the thoughts of Rudolph and Sanders.

"Money back then [in the early '70s] still wasn't a big deal," White said. "In the years I played, first place paid $20,000. I remember I finished in eighth place at Disney World one year and I think I won $1,700. That kind of money wasn't enough to catch Lew Oehmig's interest.

"But he had the game to play out there. He wouldn't have been an Arnold Palmer, one of those guys who could have come from six shots behind and win. But he would have been a guy like Gene Littler—hit it down the middle and on the green. He would have been a contender."

Erie Ball, who as the head pro at Farmington Country Club gave a young Oehmig lessons when he played for the University of Virginia, played with most of the game's greats and competed in every major championship. He knows what it would have taken to succeed on the tour when Oehmig was in his prime.

"Lew could easily have gone pro had he wanted to," Ball said. "He wasn't as long off the tee as some of the pros of the day, but that wouldn't have mattered. He was good enough to play professional golf."

Sanders isn't the only noted touring pro who shares that opinion. Sam Snead above all others knew Oehmig could play, having lost money to his old friend on occasion. Gene Littler and Oehmig tied for second in the Bing Crosby Pro-Am in 1965. And Arnold Palmer, a long-time friend and business associate, saw plenty of Oehmig's game.

"Lew Oehmig has been a very fine player over the years," Palmer said. "I would assume that he would have done very well had he chosen to pursue a pro career. As I said, he was a very fine player."

Oehmig has heard those kinds of comments all his life, but reflecting on his long career, he has no regrets. And he can be secure in the knowledge that when he played against some of the great players in golf history—Snead, Byron Nelson, Ben Hogan, Palmer and on and on—his game always measured up.

"I had a long career in amateur golf," Oehmig said. "But I don't think back to what I could have done [on the tour]. Because I won my share of tournaments at the amateur level. I had some success in the business world. And I had a wonderful wife and two sons whom I'm so proud of. I've been blessed in so many ways. I wouldn't change a thing. Not one thing."

SIGNIFICANT GOLF CHAMPIONSHIPS
WON BY LEW OEHMIG

UNITED STATES
SENIOR AMATEUR
 1972   1985
 1976

INTERNATIONAL
SENIOR CHAMPIONSHIP
 1976

TENNESSEE AMATEUR
 1937   1955
 1949   1962
 1951   1970
 1952   1971

TENNESSEE
SENIOR AMATEUR
 1968   1973
 1970   1981
 1971   1982
 1972

TENNESSEE SENIOR PGA
 1986

NATIONAL
INTERCOLLEGIATE
TOURNAMENT
CO-MEDALIST
 1937
 (University of Virginia)

CHATTANOOGA
METRO MEN'S AMATEUR
 1934   1951
 1939   1955
 1948   1978
 1949

HONORS

UNITED STATES
GOLF ASSOCIATION
BOB JONES AWARD
 1994

UNITED STATES
WALKER CUP
(non-playing captain)
 1977

TENNESSEE SPORTS
HALL OF FAME
 1973

SOUTHERN GOLF
ASSOCIATION
HALL OF FAME
 1981

TENNESSEE GOLF
HALL OF FAME
 1990

CHATTANOOGA
OLD TIMERS
SPORTS HALL OF FAME
 1974